Cambridge Elements

Elements in Politics and Society in Southeast Asia

edited by
Edward Aspinall
Australian National University
Meredith L. Weiss
University at Albany, SUNY

THAILAND

Contestation, Polarization, and Democratic Regression

Prajak Kongkirati
Thammasat University

CAMBRIDGE
UNIVERSITY PRESS

Shaftesbury Road, Cambridge CB2 8EA, United Kingdom

One Liberty Plaza, 20th Floor, New York, NY 10006, USA

477 Williamstown Road, Port Melbourne, VIC 3207, Australia

314–321, 3rd Floor, Plot 3, Splendor Forum, Jasola District Centre, New Delhi – 110025, India

103 Penang Road, #05–06/07, Visioncrest Commercial, Singapore 238467

Cambridge University Press is part of Cambridge University Press & Assessment, a department of the University of Cambridge.

We share the University's mission to contribute to society through the pursuit of education, learning and research at the highest international levels of excellence.

www.cambridge.org
Information on this title: www.cambridge.org/9781009517690

DOI: 10.1017/9781108565677

When citing this work, please include a reference to the DOI 10.1017/9781108565677

First published 2024

A catalogue record for this publication is available from the British Library.

ISBN 978-1-009-51769-0 Hardback
ISBN 978-1-108-46501-4 Paperback
ISSN 2515-2998 (online)
ISSN 2515-298X (print)

Thailand

Contestation, Polarization, and Democratic Regression

Elements in Politics and Society in Southeast Asia

DOI: 10.1017/9781108565677
First published online: April 2024

Prajak Kongkirati
Thammasat University

Author for correspondence: Prajak Kongkirati, prajakk@yahoo.com

Abstract: This Element aims to provide an overview of Thai politics with an up-to-date discussion of the characteristics of political regimes, political economy, and identity and mobilization that are grounded in historical analysis stretching back to the formation of the modern nation state. The thematic topics will focus on (1) the chronic instability and ever-changing nature of political regimes resulting in the failure of democratic consolidation, (2) the nexus of business and politics sustained by a patrimonial state structure, patronage politics, and political corruption, and (3) the contestation of identity and the causes and consequences of mass mobilization in the civic space and street politics.

Keywords: Thailand, authoritarianism, polarisation, democratic backsliding, coup

ISBNs: 9781009517690 (HB), 9781108465014 (PB), 9781108565677 (OC)
ISSNs: 2515-2998 (online), 2515-298X (print)

Contents

1 Introduction

In both 2006 and 2014, the Thai military deployed troops and tanks, seizing power from democratically elected governments led by business tycoon-turned-politicians Thaksin and Yingluck Shinawatra, respectively. The coup leaders justified their forceful overthrow of these governments by citing the need to quell the violent, polarized conflict between pro- and anti-Thaksin movements engulfing the country, and to protect the monarchy, considered the most sacred and integral foundation of the Thai nation. These two coups destabilized Thailand, making it one of the few nations still grappling with a democratic breakdown caused by military intervention.

In the aftermath of both coups, however, the country witnessed mass mobilization and resistance from grassroots organizations, democratic activists, and youth movements. Despite facing repression, these pro-democracy forces boldly and creatively defied the autocratic leaders who governed the country with strong-arm tactics. Progressive groups also formed vibrant political parties, contesting in elections with the hope of removing their autocratic leaders through the ballot box. While the pushback from these pro-democratic forces may not have toppled the authoritarian regime, it effectively undermined the regime's legitimacy and challenged the dominance of the Thai establishment.

This sequence of events points to the core political conundrum in contemporary Thai politics: While democracy has yet to be consolidated, authoritarians also encounter challenges in ensuring the durability of their rule. Chronic political instability is the result. This Element explores this contentious political landscape and the dynamics of continuity and change over the long term. It examines the two sides of the conundrum that contribute to the consistently contested nature of the Thai polity: On one side are strategies of elite political dominance, and elite responses to new political challenges; on the other side is the emergence and resilience of civil-society and mass movements actively involved in instigating democratic change.

This Element thus provides an overview of Thai politics spanning from the 1950s, when the monarchical-military alliance was formed, to the latest developments following the seismic 2023 elections. It delves into the characteristics of the Thai state, the country's changing political regimes, political economy, and political mobilization, all grounded in historical analysis, and with a focus on developments at the provincial level as well as the center. The political path of Thailand since the 1950s has been characterized by chronic instability and frequent regime changes. Military leaders, backed by the monarchy, have successfully orchestrated coups and devised undemocratic constitutions to prolong their rule, yet their authoritarian regimes have been at times overthrown by mass movements and occasionally weakened by electoral defeats. Power struggles pitting traditional royalist-military elites against new political forces are influenced by factors such as state structure, patronage politics, political institutional design, socioeconomic changes, the evolving nature of electoral competitions, and ideological contestation.

Historically, the absence of external forces, such as direct colonial rule or foreign occupation, thwarted the emergence of mass nationalist movements seen in neighboring countries like Vietnam, Indonesia, the Philippines, and Myanmar. The lack of external political intervention facilitated the perpetuation of a social and political order dominated by the royal-military-bureaucratic alliance. The potent partnership between the monarchy and the military was solidified during the Cold War, with support from American administrations seeking the backing of Thai elites in combating communism in the region. Since the 1950s, the royal-military alliance has evolved into the most influential political force in Thailand, maintaining its dominance through various means, including repression, institutional manipulation, and the co-optation of opposition forces. Periodically, the supremacy of royal-military elites has faced challenges from emerging political forces arising due to socioeconomic changes and ideological shifts.

Mass politics, led by an alliance of students, peasants, and laborers, emerged relatively late in the 1970s, driven by new ideologies and structural socioeconomic changes. A pivotal moment for Thai popular nationalism unfolded when the so-called "people's constitution" was established following the financial crisis in 1997, significantly transforming the power structure and economic landscape of the kingdom. This event enabled the ascent of a populist party led by business tycoon Thaksin Shinawatra, whose highly responsive yet illiberal governments resulted in political turbulence and profound political polarization. The counteractions of anti-Thaksin elites, involving mass mobilization, the judicialization of politics, and military coups, plunged Thailand into a phase of persistent violent conflict and political instability.

This Element is structured in five sections. The first section explores the emergence and evolution of the royal-military political alliance from the late 1950s to 1997. It scrutinizes how these traditional elites navigate shifts in society, political opposition, and challenges posed by the rise of new political actors to uphold their authority. The second section investigates the political reconfiguration that emerged after the 1997 economic crisis, marked by the ascent of Thaksin and his populist party, which significantly reshaped Thai politics. The third section delves into the origins and repercussions of the polarized conflict triggered by the 2006 coup, which was orchestrated by royal-military elites to remove Thaksin and his political network from power. This event marked the onset of the era of color-coded conflict, the decay of democratic institutions, and violent political upheaval. The fourth section elucidates the political struggle spanning from the 2014 coup to the 2023 elections, when royal-military elites sought to consolidate their power by undermining electoral democracy and manipulating democratic processes. In response, the pro-democracy movement countered through street protests and electoral challenges. The elections of 2019 and 2023 pointed to significant change and signaled the beginning of a new phase of struggle to establish a more democratic political order under the new monarch. The concluding section encapsulates the entire argument and deliberates on the trajectory of politics as well as the future prospects of democracy in Thailand.

2 Consolidation, Contestation, and Co-optation: The Royal-Military Alliance and Its Opposition

From the late 1950s to 1973, during the Cold War era, the monarchical-military alliance was the dominant political force in the kingdom. Military leaders intervened in politics through coups, establishing a robust military authoritarian regime that governed society with an expanding bureaucratic apparatus. Supported by the US, Military General Sarit Thanarat revived the monarchy to legitimize his autocratic rule and unite the masses against the communist threat. Relying on coercive force, military elites quelled dissidents and manipulated the constitution, political parties, and electoral processes to maintain their power. However, rapid economic development during this period led to dramatic social changes, fostering the emergence of university students as a new politically influential social stratum.

In the 1970s, mass mobilization led by students posed a significant challenge to military rule. Under military rule, the monarchy accumulated power and became an influential political actor. The 1973 student uprising ushered in a democratic transition and an era of mass politics. Various groups, including labor unions, peasant movements, and the business class, participated in expanding the political landscape and opening the contest for power. From the 1980s to the 1990s, a semi-democratic regime emerged as a settled political order, featuring a power-sharing arrangement between military and business elites under the hegemony of the charismatic monarch. Influential business-people entered politics to safeguard and enhance their interests. Under the framework of parliamentary democracy and the persistence of electoral politics, ambitious business actors, both in Bangkok and provincial areas, established political parties and gained significant access to state power. Elections became an increasingly important pathway to power. However, key ministries pertaining to national security and the premiership remained under the control of the military and royalist elites. Despite encountering challenges and opposition following the democratic transition in 1973, the royal-military alliance sustained its dominance through repression, the influence of a semi-democratic constitution, and the co-optation of businesspeople-turned-politicians (Asa 2021; Likhit 1988).

The Administrative Patrimonial State, Electoral Authoritarianism, and Electoral Manipulation (Pre-1973)

After the administrative reforms of King Chulalongkorn, Rama V (1853–1910) in the late nineteenth century, the Thai state gradually succeeded in centralizing political administration and monopolizing the use of force with the introduction of a modern army. The 1932 People's Party revolution, which overthrew the absolute monarchy, caused a radical regime change, bringing about a constitutional democracy. The post-revolution regimes, however, inherited a centralized, patrimonial state structure. Intra-elite conflict between rival ideological factions dominated the Thai polity during 1932–1947, and rival factions used the state apparatus to eliminate and weaken opponents (Anderson 1990; Kasian 2001). After 1947, the military became the dominant political force under over a quarter century of military regimes. Under these regimes, state security personnel perpetrated violence against dissidents, students, farmers, labor union leaders, suspected communists, and progressive politicians. This military era saw the most intense period of state-sponsored murders. The 1973 student-led uprising toppled the military government and ushered in a democratic transition. The fledgling democratic period lasted for only three years before royal-military elites and right-wing groups crushed the student–farmer–labor movements in a major massacre in 1976, ending the short period of democratic exuberance (Anderson 1977).

During 1933–1973, Thailand held nine general elections. All electoral contests were peaceful, not because governments provided effective security, but because there was no genuine competition. The governments controlled the electoral processes and manipulated the outcomes. Lack of competition also stemmed from the fact that elections were not the primary mechanisms for assuming power in Thailand prior to 1973. Instead, elite factions used military coups to control state power. Once in control, they conducted elections merely as political rituals to legitimize their administrations.

Writing in the 1960s, major scholars characterized Thailand's post-1932 political structure as a "bureaucratic polity," in which power exclusively resided and was contested within the bureaucracy (Riggs 1966). Comparatively speaking, the Thai polity in the pre-1973 period had many parallels with other countries classified as "patrimonial administrative states" – denoting political systems in which the bureaucratic elite or "political aristocracy" was the predominant social force and countervailing forces from civil society were weak.[1] Nevertheless, it is crucial to underscore that in Thailand's patrimonial administrative state, the military exercised the most influence, not civilian bureaucrats. To conflate the military and bureaucracy, as Riggs (1966) did, was a serious error. Under Thailand's successive authoritarian regimes, military elites enriched themselves by plundering public resources and extracting rents from a weak business class. They monopolized and/or nationalized businesses and industries for personal gain, and used their political influence to protect their profitable illegal enterprises (gambling, drugs, natural resource exploitation, etc.). Businesspeople who wanted government contracts and business licenses had to establish close connections with generals, appoint them to company boards, or pay them bribes (Hewison 1989; Skinner 1957; Suehiro 1989).

Under patrimonial administrative states, electoral competition has no real significance because elective posts have limited power. In Thailand, first of all, military elites circumscribed the scope and jurisdiction of elective office. They allowed voters to fill the House with elected MPs, but kept the administrative center of power away from these MPs. Before 1973, no constitution required that the prime minister or cabinet members be elected. Most constitutions allowed bureaucrats to assume cabinet positions while retaining their official posts. Therefore, Thai cabinets in the 1932–1973 period were dominated by civil servants and military officers, as well as technocrats.[2] Elected constituency MPs and businesspeople rarely took up administrative posts (a situation that changed dramatically in the late 1970s). Through this strategy of cutting representatives from the decision-making process, bureaucratic leaders walled off the policy arena from democratic interference. They also curbed elected politicians' legislative power by filling half of the assembly with appointed MPs, who had authority equal to that of their elected counterparts, and by having the Senate fully appointed by the prime minister (as in the 1947 and 1949 constitutions). Government leaders appointed assemblymen and senators from their personal networks, strengthening their regime with loyal friends and

[1] The term "patrimonial administrative state" comes from Thomas Callaghy's work on Zaire (Callaghy 1984, chapter 1). The term was borrowed and further developed by Hutchcroft (1998) to describe the Thai state before 1973.

[2] Only the 1946 and 1949 constitutions stipulated that cabinet members could not simultaneously hold bureaucratic posts. These two constitutions were, however, short lived, and, in practice, all prime ministers still recruited ministers from the civil service.

supporters.[3] In the pre-1973 period, elected MPs thus had no real administrative or legislative power. Consequently, leading businesspeople and provincial elites had few incentives to run in elections. The backgrounds of elected MPs in the early period after 1932 were mostly retired civil servants, teachers, or lawyers, or supporters of the People's Party. With almost nothing at stake, electoral contests were unaggressive. Voter turnout was very low, averaging 40 percent of eligible voters (Prajak 2013).

The real site of power contestation was in the military and other parts of the state apparatus, where elites fought for control of perks and privileges. The higher the position to which an official could ascend, the more manpower, budgetary authority, and rents they could control. Thai ruling elites enhanced their power through the expansion of their organizations. Bureaucracies were thus large and constantly expanding. Extra-bureaucratic forces, in contrast, were weak and diminished as state elites deliberately suppressed, emasculated, or destroyed them. Election-related institutions were poorly developed. Political party legislation, allowing rights and freedom of party association and legalizing party organizations, was not passed until 1955. Most parties established during 1932–1973 centered on and evolved around prominent political figures. Parties were ad hoc and short-lived organizations created to support individuals' political ambitions in competition with their immediate rivals. No party had mass support, a clear voter base, or a well-developed party organization, and most disbanded immediately after their leader's political demise (Murashima, Nakharin, and Somkiat 1991).

Over a long period, from 1932 to 1973 (except for the post-war years, 1945–1947), the Thai patrimonial administrative state oscillated between closed authoritarianism and electoral authoritarianism.[4] Under closed authoritarianism (the Sarit Thanarat government of 1958–1963 and the Thanom Kittikachorn governments of 1963–1969 and 1971–1973), military rulers severely restricted civil liberties and prohibited all democratic institutions. Dictatorial leaders did not try to legitimize themselves by attaining popular support. They did not invest in holding elections, even sham ones. During the electoral authoritarian periods (1947–1957, 1969–1971), governments neither practiced liberal democracy nor operated full-blown authoritarianism. Instead, leaders allowed limited space for political participation and competition through electoral

[3] Only the 1946 constitution required the senate be indirectly elected (voters elected an electoral college which then elected the senators).

[4] From 1945 to 1947, Pridi Banomyong's civilian faction dominated the administration and assembly. Pridi and his supporters passed the 1946 constitution, regarded as one of the most democratic constitutions in Thai history, eliminating appointed MPs. A brief democratic interlude ended in November 1947 when the army staged a coup and toppled the Pridi-backed government.

processes. By holding periodic elections in such systems, rulers "try to obtain at least a semblance of democratic legitimacy, hoping to satisfy external as well as internal actors. At the same time, by placing those elections under tight authoritarian controls they try to cement their continued hold on power," with the ultimate goal being to "reap the fruits of electoral legitimacy without running the risks of democratic uncertainty" (Schedler 2002, 36–37).[5]

In general, in such systems, ruling elites have various tools (legal and illegal) to deprive voters of genuine electoral choices, including excluding opposition candidates from the electoral arena, restricting access to information and resources, disenfranchising some groups of voters, and committing electoral fraud.[6] Thailand's authoritarian rulers used many such techniques. For example, the February 1957 election, known as "the dirty election," was regarded as the most corrupt in Thai history. This election was held when Premier Phibun (Plaek Phibunsongkhram) wanted to enhance the legitimacy of his long-standing rule domestically and internationally, and to use the democratic credentials gained from the election for greater leverage over other elite factions. To ensure a decisive victory, government leaders mobilized state networks to support government-backed candidates. They deployed police and soldiers to intimidate voters and coerced opposing candidates to withdraw. False registrations, ballot tampering, and vote rigging abounded. Nationwide, the government-backed party won decisively (Prajak 2013).

The government's brazen electoral fraud led to student protests. On March 2, 1957, students led a march denouncing the government party and accusing it of rigging the results. Using electoral fraud as a pretext, rivals of Phibun, Sarit Thanarat and his followers staged a coup on September 16, 1957, toppling the Phibun government and introducing a military absolutist regime. The Sarit administration (1958–1963) revoked the constitution and ruled the country by military decrees, dissolving the assembly and banning all political parties, civic associations, and elections. Military elites formulated the concept of "Thai-style democracy" to justify their autocratic rule by contending that liberal democracy, rooted in Western culture, was unsuitable for Thai society. They asserted that Thailand's traditions favored harmonious, orderly society over contentious, divisive politics. The best form of governance for Thailand, Sarit argued, was a paternalistic system led by a strong charismatic leader. Distinguished by its autocratic conduct, Sarit's political regime is appropriately labeled "despotic paternalism" (Thak 1979). This political model left a lasting impact, serving as

[5] For more conceptual and empirical discussion regarding electoral authoritarianism, see Levitsky and Way (2010), Brownlee (2007), and Case (2010) on Southeast Asia.

[6] Schedler (2002, 36–50) provides a list of electoral manipulations used around the world. Case (2006, 95–112) discusses Asian experience.

a blueprint for subsequent generations of military leaders to emulate and implement when they assumed power.

As a provincial army officer, Sarit also revived and popularized the institution of the monarchy to lend legitimacy to his rule. Sarit never subscribed to the principles of constitutional democratic rule as had the military leaders involved in the People Party's revolution. He was aware that traditional institutions like the monarchy had symbolic power and political capital that he could use. Sarit's strategy generated a crucial turning point that significantly changed the nature of Thai politics and made the monarchical-military alliance the most powerful force in the kingdom. The influence of the monarchy, waning after the 1932 revolution, was restored. A loose network of royalist nobles, conservative intellectuals, and bureaucrats was established to offer political advice and services to the young King Bhumibol Adulyadej (1927–2016). Step by step, the king, with the support of his royalist network and allied military leaders, accumulated political capital, expanded his scope of power, and became involved in political affairs (Charnvit 2020; McCargo 2005; Thak 1979).

After Sarit died in 1963, power passed to his political heir Thanom, who extended military rule for another decade with the support of the monarchy and the US government. During the Vietnam War, the United States administration extended substantial financial and military assistance in return for Thailand's support in the conflict. This arrangement helped reinforce and perpetuate military rule. The US government played a crucial role in promoting and elevating the monarchy as the unified symbol of the nation, viewing the royal family as a valuable political asset in the fight against communism (Nattapol 2020).

Governments also used security forces arbitrarily to crack down on anti-government activists. A large group of politicians and activists were imprisoned without charges, and some were executed, and those who managed to escape were forced to go underground or into exile. The Thai political system was cleansed of radical, progressive groups. Therefore, when Thanom called an election in 1969 – under growing domestic and international pressure, having had no election for eleven years – his Sahaprachathai Party (United Thai People's Party) faced no real challenge. Government electoral fraud and malpractice were pervasive, and the Sahaprachathai Party won the election handily. Military elites were unified and had dominant control; therefore, no post-election protests occurred (Prajak 2013).

In short, under autocratic rule prior to 1973, military elites controlled state power using coercive force and electoral manipulation. The administrative patrimonial state structure empowered and enriched the military and civilian bureaucratic elites while suppressing civilian politicians and civil society.

A major political transformation was coming, however; after 1973, elections and extra-bureaucratic forces became increasingly important.

Thailand's Democratic Transition, Political Polarization, and State-Sponsored Violence, 1973–1976

The Thanom regime was brought to an end by the mass uprising led by students on October 14, 1973. The Sarit–Thanom administration's rapid capitalist development inadvertently set the stage for student mobilization. During 1957–1973, Thailand underwent significant social changes, including urbanization, expansion of higher education, and heightened exposure to mass media and foreign cultures. University students became a prominent social force. Frustrated by oppressive rule and inspired by youth movements abroad, Thai students actively engaged in national politics, challenging the authoritarian regime. The turning point occurred in October 1973 when police arrested students and intellectuals peacefully advocating an end to autocratic rule and the establishment of a democratic constitution. This event triggered public outrage and street demonstrations. On October 13–14, 1973, half a million people joined a student-led demonstration to demand a constitution and Thanom's resignation. During the demonstration, soldiers fired into the demonstrators, killing 77 and wounding 857.

Prior to the uprising, the monarchy was acutely aware of public anger at corruption and abuse of power; accordingly, the king started to criticize the Thanom government and show moral support to student protestors. The intervention of the king on the side of the student movement and certain military elites (Thanom's rivals), plus the persistence of protest after the initial killings, rendered military suppression ineffective. The presence of the monarchy as an autonomous power center within the regime, alongside persistent elite conflict, was vital to the students' successful toppling of the military dictatorship.

Divisions within the authoritarian regime can be traced back to the late 1960s. The most significant divide was within the army, but there were also signs of tension between the army and the palace. In general, the king endorsed military rule, believing strong rule was needed to uphold the monarchy and defeat communism. Nevertheless, he frequently criticized government policies when he thought they had gone in the wrong direction, and he did so more strongly in the early 1970s. Amid the political crisis, the palace dissociated itself from the unpopular and corrupt Thanom government to safeguard the public image of the king. Following Thanom's downfall, the king and royalist network effectively seized this opportunity of regime transition to assert a more active role for the monarchy in the political arena (Prajak 2012; Thongchai 2016).

The 1973 uprising ushered in a highly unstable interim period of civilian democracy. Under the government of Prime Minister Sanya Thammasak (1973–1974), a royalist judge, the country witnessed greater political participation than in any other period before or since. Press censorship virtually disappeared, and the democratic 1974 constitution was promulgated, creating a more open political environment. Trade unions rapidly formed, pressing a host of demands through strikes and marches. New peasant organizations urged land reform. Even high-school children demanded the expulsion of hated principals. Several left-leaning and socialist parties were established to compete in the general elections (Anderson 1977; see Haberkorn 2011 on peasant movements).

After its success in toppling the authoritarian regime, the student movement maintained pressure on the new civilian government to sustain democracy, and it also formed an alliance with peasants and workers to fight for social and economic justice. This progressive alliance threatened the traditional beliefs, economic interests, and political power of the privileged class, including army and bureaucratic leaders, business tycoons, rural landlords, and royalists. Ruling groups strongly felt their privileges and power were in danger. Some factions in the army were particularly alarmed by the new tripartite alliance's radical ideas, which challenged the military's concept of a controlled and orderly society, and their national security policy. The student movement's campaign for the withdrawal of US troops from Thailand was especially threatening (Anderson 1977).

Under military dictatorship, government officials had been accustomed to exercising arbitrary authority and enjoyed virtual immunity from criticism. After the uprising, they found themselves being criticized and questioned by the poor and the disadvantaged. Business entrepreneurs could no longer take for granted the extremely cheap labor that the military regime had guaranteed. Now, they had to negotiate with labor unions, which were supported by the student movement and left-wing politicians. Landlords also were worried by peasant demands for land reform. Many elites believed the new civilian governments were too weak, and were incapable of protecting their interests. Accordingly, these elites ventured into extra-parliamentary tactics. They created right-wing militias and paramilitary groups, with leadership and logistical support provided by military elites, to disrupt the progressive coalition. State security force personnel carried out a series of clandestine assassinations targeting leaders of peasant, labor, and student organizations. Confrontational and violent tactics by rightists, combined with government inaction, eventually debilitated the student movement (Bowie 1997; Prajak 2008).

The escalation of violence led to political turmoil and ended with a brutal massacre of students on October 6, 1976.[7] According to police records, forty-three people were killed, several hundred injured, and over three thousand arrested on that day. One army faction staged a coup, taking power from the elected civilian government that evening, terminating three years of popular democracy and progressive mobilization, turning Thai politics back toward dictatorship. Thailand's experience after the 1973 uprising confirms the proposition that democratic transition triggered by abrupt regime collapse can produce a fragile and violent period of rule (O'Donnell, Schmitter, and Whitehead 1986, 11). Nonetheless, it was not the mobilization of progressive reformers that was responsible for the breakdown of the democratic transition, but the violence perpetrated by the royal-military-bureaucratic elites. After 1976, unprecedented numbers of radical students, intellectuals, and political activists took up armed struggle, joining the Communist Party of Thailand (CPT) and then waging guerrilla warfare in jungle areas – a deadly civil war that lasted for almost a decade and killed thousands of people.

Parliamentary Democracy and Electoral Competition under a Patrimonial State (1976–1997)

From 1979 to 1996, Thailand held eight general elections, experienced three coup attempts (one successful in 1991 and two failed, in 1981 and 1985), had two constitutions (the 1978 constitution and the 1991 constitution), and witnessed a large demonstration in 1992 against an unelected military prime minister. In rural areas, after the 1976 massacre, the CPT grew stronger and gained momentum. The government attacked the CPT using enormous resources, but it was not until the mid-1980s that the CPT collapsed and no longer posed a political or security threat to ruling elites. These two decades between the 1976 massacre and the 1997 economic crisis were an unstable period in Thai politics. Nevertheless, it was during this period that a new political order emerged. Parliamentary democracy was steadily established to replace the preceding pattern of authoritarian bureaucratic politics (interrupted briefly by the 1991 coup)[8] and the balance of political power over time shifted

[7] That morning, units of the Border Patrol Police from several provinces, units of police in Bangkok, along with right-wing paramilitary groups invaded Thammasat University, where 5000 people had gathered peacefully all night to protest the return of Thanom. They fired rockets, handguns, and anti-tank missiles into the university. A handful of students who tried to escape were brutally lynched, raped, or burnt alive (Thongchai 2020).

[8] On February 23, 1991, generals Sunthorn Kongsompong and Suchinda Kraprayoon led a coup that ousted the elected government of Chatichai Choonhavan. Despite his earlier pledge not to seek the premiership, the junta leader, Suchinda, appointed himself prime minister. In response, pro-democracy groups initiated demonstrations in May 1992, demanding Suchinda's resignation

from military-bureaucratic elites to metropolitan and provincial capitalists.[9] Electoral politics became more significant as the primary channel for acquiring political position, privilege, patronage, and wealth. This changing political environment provided both opportunities and incentives for business leaders and local elites to enter politics (Anderson 1990).

For a brief period after October 6, 1976, Thai society was under the civilian dictatorship of Thanin Kraivixien, an anti-communist lawyer trusted by the king. Thanin pursued authoritarian policies undermining all democratic institutions, including elections and political parties. Thanin's ultra-royalist and conservative rule alienated nearly all societal groups, business elites, and extra-bureaucratic forces that had emerged since the Sarit Thanarat era of rapid economic development. These groups had become a formidable force since the mid-1970s and demanded wider political participation. They viewed the Thanin government's authoritarian turn as unacceptable. They criticized Thanin's rule and, in less than a year, Thanin lost public support and was overthrown by military officers on October 20, 1977. The coup group appointed General Kriengsak Chamanand, a more reform-minded army leader, as the new prime minister. The Kriengsak administration was aware of the changing political landscape in which the bureaucracy could no longer rule the country without accommodating the interests of influential groups – especially from private business – who wanted an open parliamentary system. Kriengsak appointed constitutional experts and technocrats to draft a new constitution to pave the way for the next general election. Against this backdrop, the 1978 constitution was a social contract between two groups of elites, the old military-bureaucratic leaders and the new business elites, to share power under an agreed parliamentary platform (Chai-anan 1989; Likhit 1988).

The mode of political compromise and power-sharing was manifested in several articles of the 1978 constitution. The constitution established a bicameral National Assembly, consisting of an elected House of Representatives and an appointed Senate. The lower house had the power to submit a motion of no-confidence against the government; meanwhile, the Senate had statutory power to oversee and block the lower house's legislation. Most importantly, the constitution stipulated that it was not necessary for the prime minister and cabinet members to be elected, allowing civilian bureaucrats

and a democratic constitution. The protesters faced violent suppression. Recognizing Suchinda's extreme unpopularity, the king eventually intervened to halt the bloodshed. Under mounting pressure, Suchinda resigned on May 24, 1992. This event was popularly known as "the May 1992 Bloodshed" (Callahan 1998).

9 For general political context of the 1980s and 1990s, see Anderson (1990) and Ockey (1992). On the political economy of the Thai state during this era, see Brown (2004), Hewison (1989), and Pasuk and Baker (1995).

and army leaders to take positions without standing for election. Those who drafted the constitution designed the Senate-by-appointment and unelected prime ministership to retain power bases for the military and traditional elites within the parliamentary system.[10] Under the 1978 constitution, in which elected and unelected power holders coexisted side by side in the assembly and government, the Thai polity was popularly labeled "a semi-democratic system" (Chai-anan 1989, 31).

The key figure overseeing this political arrangement was General Prem Tinsulanonda, who was prime minister during 1980–1988. Prem wielded power for eight years without contesting in elections or affiliating with any political party. A military officer renowned for his role in combating the communist insurgency, upholding an uncorrupted image, and displaying unwavering loyalty to the royal family, Prem earned high trust from the palace. Since both the military and the monarchy supported Prem, every political party recognized it was necessary for him to head the cabinet, regardless of electoral outcome. Prem played a crucial role in facilitating the transition to domination for traditional elites, countering the communists, accommodating the more vocal business class, and subduing ambitious young military officers within the army. It was during Prem's tenure that the alliance between the monarchy and military was solidified, with the military becoming a loyal subordinate to the king (Chambers and Napisa 2016; McCargo 2005).

The change in relative power between the state and business interests occurred under the overarching structure of a patrimonial state. Once democratization began in the early 1980s, the character of this patrimonial state was largely sustained. What changed was the relative strength of bureaucratic and business elites and the direction of rent extraction. Under previous military authoritarian regimes, bureaucratic elites extracted rents from a weak business class, while under the semi-democratic regime, a business class started to extract rents from a weakened bureaucracy (cf. Anek 1992; Prajak 2013).

In this sense, from the late 1970s to the 1990s, the Thai polity experienced a major shift in the nature of power relations. At the beginning of this period, Thailand had a political system in which the military-bureaucratic elite was dominant. By the 1990s, it had gradually become a "patrimonial oligarchic state" in which the business elite was the most influential social force, having "an economic base largely independent of the state apparatus, but the state nonetheless plays a central role in the process of wealth accumulation"

[10] The 1978 constitution also had a temporary clause, stipulating that within the first four years of the constitution's usage, the senate would have equal power to the Lower House, including power to issue a no-confidence motion, and that civil servants and military officers could assume the premiership and cabinet posts while retaining their bureaucratic positions.

(Hutchcroft 1998, 52). The intensity and speed of change from "patrimonial administrative state" to "patrimonial oligarchic state" was intermittent, with parts of the traditional bureaucratic elite resisting this transformation. But the combination of patrimonialism and parliamentary democracy offered major incentives to business elites to become involved in electoral competition. Their goal was to maximize their access to the centralized state machinery, the major channel for rent-seeking opportunities. Public office provided an avenue for politico-business actors to access lucrative licenses, permits, concessions, quotas, loans, and power to manipulate laws and state regulations. The stakes of winning elections were thus higher than ever as victory gave capitalists access to state coffers. In this changed environment, major business leaders grasped electoral opportunities at both national and local levels (Arghiros 2001; Nishizaki 2011; Ockey 2000). With higher stakes, electoral competition became fiercer.

The prevalence of self-serving business elites, especially provincial bosses, in politics had adverse effects on the advancement and quality of Thai democracy. With factional politics heavily influenced by these politico-business actors, the party system became fragmented, and political parties struggled to maintain political longevity. The cabinet became a venue for money politics and patronage distribution, resulting in a corrupt and ineffective coalition government.

To fully understand the politics of this era, one also needs to look at the political and economic transformation at the local level.

Local Economy and Politics: Subnational Enclaves, Rent-Seeking, and Illegal Economies

In Thailand, two types of transformation dramatically changed Thai provincial life: the shift from a rural to an industrial and service economy, which started in the 1960s, and the advent of parliamentary democracy, which began after 1973. Both the political and economic environments changed, and a new array of actors began to play a role. Economic development programs and investment started to expand into rural areas in every region, producing more jobs, factories, business services, and opportunities for local elites to develop into a capitalist class. Nevertheless, the pace of provincial economic development was slow. The gap between the Bangkok-based economy and provincial economies was staggeringly large. Even in the 1990s, scholars characterized the provincial economies as "backward," with three dominant characteristics: "small-scale business, weak manufacturing, and few exportable manufactured products" (Ueda 1995, 87).

Generally, the provincial manufacturing sector was weak as only a very small number of local businesses had the ability to engage in modern manufacturing to "develop-high-valued and exportable new products . . . in reply to changes in the world market" (Ueda 1995, 87–88). This characterization applies to almost every province outside Bangkok. Provincial businesses had limited capital and lacked access to technology and skilled labor (mainly caused by the government's policy bias in favor of developing Bangkok as the single, dominant economic center) (Bello, Cunningham, and Li 1999; Donor and Ramsay 2000, 2003).

Even by the 1990s, industrial investment in provincial areas was limited and did not contribute significantly to provincial economic development. Only a few local business elites had invested in manufacturing, concentrating on agricultural products or low-skilled and labor-intensive manufacturing. More attractive to provincial entrepreneurs was "unproductive profit-seeking activity" or, in other words, rent-seeking.[11]

Among Thai provincial elites, the two most popular rent-seeking activities, which required very low skill and technology but gave high profits, were extractive natural resource businesses (logging, mining, quarries, etc.) and businesses in which strict government regulations provided opportunities for monopolistic profits (such as liquor or cigarette dealerships, tobacco curing, buses, gas stations, and construction). Public-sector construction was particularly important. According to data from the early 2000s, seventy-five political families in seven different parties had strong economic bases in construction. These families were very successful in elections and dominated parliament. In the 2001 election, for example, seventy-nine MPs (or 15.8 percent of the assembly) were members of families tied to these construction cartels (Noppanan 2006). Construction was attractive not only for its large income and profits, but also because provincial elites could use government construction projects to build clientelistic networks by allocating projects to business allies, relatives, and subordinates, and gain popularity from locals by bringing development to their region.

Since natural resource extraction, dealerships, and construction all require government contracts obtained through political connections, these businesses created incentives for provincial businesspeople to step into politics. Moreover, since these businesses are monopolistic by nature, they created a zero-sum game for stakeholders. A situation arose in which wealth accumulation benefited from political connections, and acquiring and sustaining political power in turn required considerable wealth. Provincial businesspeople sitting in the

[11] For a discussion of rent-seeking in Thailand, see Thanee and Pasuk (2008).

House gained influence over the allocation of patronage and rents and, of course, over the policymaking process; they became aware that their votes mattered to sustain weak, multi-party coalition governments.

Generally, provincial business elites focused their investments in their own province or, at best, on a regional-scale (Chaiyon and Olarn 2008; Viengrat 2008). Their provinces were their business "enclaves," places where they could not afford to lose control. As a result, provincial business elites had higher stakes in elections than other types of candidates. In fact, the higher the degree of candidates' involvement in rent-seeking, the fiercer the election became. The most dangerous situation occurred when rival bosses competed over the limited number of parliamentary seats. Business and political conflict intertwined, with business rivals becoming political enemies, and electoral competition becoming wars of monopoly and survival (Prajak 2016c).

Another activity attractive to provincial elites was the high-risk, high-return illegal economy. The scale of Thailand's illegal economy is large and extends across a wide range of enterprises, including drug trafficking, goods smuggling, contraband trading, illicit logging, prostitution, and gambling. Studies show that since the mid-1980s, the illegal economy has rapidly developed side by side with Thailand's economic growth. During 1993–1995, according to (conservative) estimates, illegal activities "generated 286–457 thousand million baht of value-added per annum . . . [,] equivalent to 8–13% of GNP" (Pasuk, Sungsidh, and Nualnoi 1998, 7–8). Provincial bosses liked illegal businesses because they enabled them to finance their clientelistic networks by providing employment and income for local people. However, illegal economic activity was high risk. To reduce the risk, provincial bosses acquired political protection, either by building political connections or winning elections to obtain power.

In summary, with empowered parliamentary politics and rapid economic growth, rent-seeking and illegal business became connected to electoral politics. Their interconnectedness created conditions for high-stakes elections, which led to uncompromising competition and even the use of violence in securing elective posts. The next section discusses the key characteristics of local power structures.

Terrain of Power Contestation

Although rent-allocating and protection-dispensing occurred in the capital, the primary battlegrounds were in the provinces. In order to make a political impression nationally, provincial elites had to build a solid local political base. Some locals launched their political careers in local administrative offices (district, municipal, and provincial councils) before running for a national legislative position. Local political families usually put their relatives in these offices so they could acquire political experience and create local power bases. However, prior to decentralization (implemented in 1997), these local offices operated with only a small budget and limited political mandate, and were largely controlled by bureaucrats. Prominent people viewed them as stepping stones to a more powerful and lucrative career as an MP.

After the 1979 election, each province witnessed growing political prominence of provincial business-cum-political elites, popularly called as *jao pho* (godfathers) (Ockey 1993; Sombat 2000). Even though the local economic environment provided incentives for business elites to engage in politics, not all businesspeople entered politics. Those who refrained were mostly those whose businesses did not depend primarily on political connections or coercive power. Many were scared off by the volatile nature of provincial politics. Families or individuals who were active in politics, in contrast, generally ran businesses that needed political power to enhance and protect their wealth. These so-called "godfather figures" engaged in violence in elections. They employed hired gunmen and local thugs to assassinate rivals and intimidate voters. Throughout the 1979–1996 period, an estimated 100 candidates and vote canvassers were killed in electoral competitions (Prajak 2013, 122).

The power of local godfathers depended on their ability to monopolize the local economy and political system. Each province had (and generally still has) more than one figure or family with the ambition to amass wealth and power at the expense of others. The boss who succeeded was generally the one who was most competent and cunning in exercising their financial, political, and coercive resources to weaken and/or eliminate their opponents. Securing a power monopoly, in certain circumstances, involved violence.

Apart from challenges from rivals, provincial bureaucratic elites contested godfathers' power. Godfathers still had to operate and exercise their power within the context of an archaic provincial bureaucratic structure that dated back to the absolute monarchy. It would thus be misleading to think of these bosses as local warlords or patrimonial lords who roamed freely in their territories, operating like a parastate that controlled all activities and resources in their area.[12] Instead of functioning under a failed or dysfunctional state, Thai provincial bosses operated under local power structures that had previously been controlled by bureaucratic elites: the provincial governor, provincial department heads, district chiefs, sub-district heads, village heads, as well as

[12] For example, Philippine local bosses were able to possess enormous economic power and assume "quasi-military and quasi-judicial functions in their localities" (Hutchcroft 1998, 43; see also McCoy 1993). For the even more striking power of African warlords, see Reno (1998) and Weinstein (2006).

provincial police chiefs and military commanders. Provincial bosses needed to negotiate, cooperate, and/or sometimes strive against these state authorities to carve out territorial power in their localities.

Contestation between long-standing state authorities and emerging bosses manifested differently from province to province. In provinces in which two or more warring factions competed fiercely, bureaucrats enjoyed relative autonomy. In provinces completely controlled by a single boss (or one clan), bureaucrats were under the boss's thumb. Even so, it is mistaken to portray godfathers' power as ubiquitous and permanent. Often forgotten is the fact that Thai provincial bosses are a short-lived phenomenon. In contrast to Philippine political dynasties that date to the early twentieth century, most Thai political clans entered politics after 1973. Out of the ninety-seven clans active in Thai politics from 1933 to 1996 (twenty in the north, twenty-one in central, thirty-one in northeast, seventeen in Bangkok, and eight in the south), only eighteen had entered politics before the 1960s. And by 1996, all but two of these old clans had withdrawn or disappeared from national politics. A clan's time in politics is relatively short: 25 percent of political families sustain power for only one or two terms of legislation, and of the 20 percent that intermittently stood in elections, only half managed to stay in power for more than two terms. Historically, their instability was caused by frequent military coups, which interrupted parliamentary institutions and the electoral process and thus their access to power at the national and local level. Their short time in politics meant these bosses were under severe pressure from both business rivals and the local state apparatus (Prajak 2016c). Moreover, by the time political clans and bosses had succeeded in climbing to the apex of power in 1996, the political and economic landscape had been transformed in a way that seriously reduced their power.

3 Economic Crisis, National Political Restructuring, and Local Power Reordering (1997–2006)

The period from 1997 to 2006 was highly transformative and turbulent for Thai politics and society. Parliamentary democracy and electoral institutions underwent a dramatic change. Initially, the new constitution and political reform produced a strong and stable civilian administration and party structure. Programmatic politics and policy-based campaigning became increasingly important in shaping electoral outcomes, even though the particularistic elements of patronage, pork, personality, and coercion persisted. Party and electoral institutions were stronger than ever, and meaningfully connected to a majority of the electorate. Direct elections at the local level enabled by decentralization helped create stronger linkages between voters and elected politicians. However, the military coup in 2006 derailed the legitimacy and development of parliamentary democracy (Surachart 2019).

The traditional royal-military-bureaucratic power alliance, apprehensive about its diminishing power but unwilling to compete electorally, employed an old-fashioned, coercive tool (the coup) to recapture state power and overthrow the popularly elected government. The 2006 coup profoundly transformed Thai politics; it polarized the country and radicalized political participation. Electoral competition became infused with a new element of ideological contestation. The changing rules, landscape, and power structure of Thai politics at the national level strongly affected local political settings, including the balance of power between political groups and families, and between national parties and local bosses. In particular, three national-level factors contributed to the transformation of Thai politics from 1997 to 2006: the 1997 constitution and its newly designed electoral system, the rise of a strong populist party led by Thaksin Shinawatra, and the 2006 military coup.

The New Electoral System and the 1997 Constitution: Changing Rules and Unintended Consequences

A movement for political reform began after the May 1992 bloodshed. Journalists, academics, and other reformers defined money politics and vote buying, as well as weak coalition governments, as core problems of Thai politics. Just as importantly, they viewed the provincial businesspeople-cum-politicians as the main culprits. Reformers deplored rural politicians, accusing them of using "dirty" money to buy votes from rural, poor, and uneducated voters and of plundering public resources to win elections and gain personal benefits. Immediately after the economic crisis of July 1997, the push for political reform galvanized support from the urban middle class, civil-society, and business elites who blamed the crisis on incompetent government run by rural politicians. Three months later, in October 1997, the legislative assembly passed a new constitution. The new constitution had two main goals: to create a capable and stable government and to eradicate vote buying and money politics (Callahan 2005; Connors 2002). An unspoken and connected goal was to prevent provincial politicians from assuming power, as had occurred earlier in the 1990s.

To curb the power of provincial politicians and money politics, the constitution drafters redesigned the electoral system, election administration, and rules for party organization (Hicken 2006; Kuhonta 2008). The new constitution replaced the Ministry of the Interior with an independent body, the Election

Commission of Thailand (ECT), as the agency tasked with administering and overseeing elections. The ECT was mandated to investigate violations of electoral laws and misconduct, and it had the power to counter electoral fraud by disqualifying candidates before or after voting day. These sweeping powers effectively made the ECT one of the key players shaping electoral results, and therefore a gatekeeper in national politics.

Apart from creating the ECT, the 1997 constitution generated several new organizations, mechanisms, and rules. For the first time in history, it provided that senators be elected directly rather than being appointed. It made voting compulsory for all eligible voters and restricted party switching, a popular practice among Thai politicians. However, the most far-reaching reform was a major overhaul of the electoral system. As part of an attempt to facilitate coherent political parties (to replace the ever-shifting coalitions self-interested provincial bosses favored), it replaced the block-vote system (used under the 1978 and 1992 constitutions) with a mixed-member system. Out of 500 House seats, 400 were elected from single-member districts on a plurality basis (or first past the post, FPTP), and another 100 were elected from a single nationwide district on a proportional basis. All political parties had to submit a list of candidates for voters to consider and to rank-order those on the party list. Each candidate had to decide whether they ran for a constituency or a party-list seat, and each voter cast one vote for their district representative and another for a party list. The constituency and party-list votes were calculated separately. The introduction of a party-list system aimed to provide an opportunity for technocrats, businesspeople, or professionals (basically, non-provincial boss-type candidates) to enter politics. It also aimed to strengthen party-building and party identity (Hicken 2007; Siripan 2006).

The Rise of the Populist Party: New Political Actors and the Goal of Political Monopolization

The economic crisis and the new constitution created incentives and opportunities for more party-oriented politics. The emergence of the Thai Rak Thai Party and its participation in national elections after 2001 dramatically changed Thailand's political landscape. The Thai Rak Thai (TRT) introduced party-based and relatively policy-oriented politics, a new style of electoral campaigning, and the ambitious goal of creating a single-party government. Electoral competition thus changed along with the relationship between parties and provincial bosses. The political changes brought about by the TRT placed provincial elites in a new socio-political environment, forcing them to adjust their strategies.

Thaksin Shinawatra (1950-), a telecommunication business tycoon-turned-politician, founded the Thai Rak Thai Party in 1998. Thaksin was born in Chiang Mai to a prominent business family, some of whose members had successful political careers. He was a police officer until 1987, after which he became a full-time businessman, making a considerable fortune after obtaining government concessions in mobile phone and satellite networks. Similar to other leading businesspeople, his connections with top military and bureaucratic officials and politicians helped his business and gave him protection. By the mid-1990s, he was a rising star entrepreneur and an advocate of economic and political reform (McCargo and Ukrist 2005; Pasuk and Baker 2004).

After the 1997 economic crisis and the promulgation of the new constitution, Thaksin launched the Thai Rak Thai Party, aiming to be the first prime minister elected in the post-reform era. The crisis created strong incentives for prominent capitalists, including Thaksin, to directly capture state power: "Business was shocked by the severity of economic slump, and by the refusal of the Democrat Party government (1997–2001) to assume any responsibility for defending domestic capital against its impact" (Thanee and Pasuk 2008, 255–256). Thaksin led a group of national-level capitalists, who were not severely damaged by the crisis, in pursuing a high-risk, high-return path of direct ownership over their own party, rather than building clientelistic relations with leading bureaucrats and politicians or sponsoring other people's parties (Thanee and Pasuk 2008). The new electoral and party systems were designed to promote strong executive power and big parties. This reorientation, in turn, facilitated Thaksin's and his allies' political ambitions.

Thaksin's strategy thus differed from those of other political oligarchs of the pre-1997 period. Rather than trying to win a plurality of votes and sharing power with other leaders in a multi-party coalition, he sought to win an absolute majority of votes and form a single-party government. In other words, he and his party strove for monopolistic control instead of the more conventional mode of sharing power. To achieve this goal, TRT recruited, as core members responsible for formulating party strategies and policies, technocrats, bankers, academics, businesspeople, retired civil servants, judges, activists, and former student leaders. But when the election approached, Thaksin called upon a different type of person, with whom he established alliances in all regions: the provincial political boss.

As a practical businessman-turned-politician, Thaksin consistently fielded top bosses in constituency seats on the understanding that the FPTP electoral system was, by and large, a candidate-centered system. The TRT party ran with a complementary, two-pronged strategy: a party-focused campaign for the party-list seats and a candidate-centered campaign for constituency seats. The party introduced a poverty-alleviation policy package, featuring universal health care, a rural debt moratorium, and a village fund to appeal to voters. Electoral results in many districts demonstrated that the popularity of the party's policies boosted the candidates' standing and assisted their win. Several of TRT's less influential candidates were able to defeat powerful bosses because of the party-policy package. It was clear, however, that personalistic strategies, such as vote buying, did not entirely disappear (Somchai 2008). The candidates of TRT who belonged to eminent political clans relied on both the party brand *and* their family networks. What was new was Thaksin and TRT's direct intervention in altering the balance of power among provincial politicians. Their large-scale financial and political support helped bosses allied with the TRT to gain the upper hand over rivals. Provincial bosses who refused to cooperate with the TRT faced difficulties in mobilizing resources and recruiting vote canvassers. Contests between bosses thus still produced violent outcomes (Prajak 2013; Prajak 2016c). Overall, Thaksin and his party disrupted existing local political markets. The massive war chest and popular policies of TRT attracted many politicians and vote canvassers. There was large-scale migration to the TRT during the run-up to the 2001 election (helped by a constitutional article which stipulated that the 2001 election would be the last in which candidates could be a party member for less than ninety days before the election). While the TRT thus built a strong political machine in a short period, its success at doing so aggravated local political divisions.

Over time, the rise of Thaksin and Thai Rak Thai weakened the standing of provincial godfathers. After winning in a landslide in 2001 and becoming a highly popular leader, Thaksin pursued a bold strategy to domesticate the power of leading provincial political bosses both within and outside his party. Within TRT, Thaksin sidelined factional leaders since he did not want any bosses to have too much control over party members. Thaksin played the classic game of divide and rule by pitting factions within his party against each other so that no single boss threatened government stability or his personal supremacy. Prominent cabinet members mainly came from his inner circle and were family-connected allies or technocrats and professionals, and Thaksin frequently rotated or reshuffled his cabinet members. With less access to ministerial posts and thus rent allocations, provincial bosses saw their position significantly decline. Certain disgruntled bosses expressed their grievances and mounted an intra-party campaign against Thaksin's strong rule, but they gained insufficient support from the public and party members.

By bypassing local political brokers, Thaksin could rely on party policies, branding, and the party machine to win votes instead of local personal networks. In short, he changed the system to serve his ambitious personal goals. In the process, however, this policy campaign helped drive a political transformation away from a pattern of provincial-boss dominated, factional politics toward a party-dominated, policy-oriented politics (Nam and Viengrat 2021).

By the end of 2003, Thaksin had succeeded in asserting absolute control over all leading bosses in his party. He became the boss of bosses. The Thaksin administration was thus the first in modern Thai history to attempt to domesticate and eliminate local bosses who had, for many decades, acted as political intermediaries in the Thai political system. Past governments, both dictatorial and democratic, had lacked the political will, legitimacy, or capacity to pursue this goal. For Thaksin, by contrast, provincial bosses posed a threat to his populist party-building, and he knew that his electoral success would be more sustainable if he did not need to rely on local godfathers.

Ironically, precisely by the time Thaksin had achieved his almost monopolistic control over electoral politics in the 2005 elections, he had rendered himself vulnerable to another sort of threat. His royal-military-bureaucratic opponents, realizing the impossibility of defeating him electorally in the monopolistic political market, resorted to non-electoral, extra-parliamentary measures to unseat him. Eventually, in 2006, the royal-military alliance staged a coup to topple Thaksin. This coup drove Thai politics into a new era, once again changing the political landscape at both national and local levels.

4 Political Crisis: Polarization, Inequality, and Violence (2006–2014)

The political ascendancy of Thaksin and his populist party prompted a backlash from the old elite. The royalist coup in 2006, orchestrated to overthrow the most popular elected government in modern Thai history, sparked a protracted political crisis. Between 2006 and 2014, Thai politics were defined by rivalry between two influential networks: the "network monarchy," centered around the charismatic monarch, drawing on a foundation of traditional moral authority, and the "Thaksin network," focused on the elected populist leader, deriving legitimacy from its popular mandate and the principle of majoritarian democracy.

This conflict also had structural causes rooted in social cleavages based on the urban–rural divide and income inequality, with the intense elite power struggle exacerbating these structural tensions. Both sides engaged in mass mobilization, employing confrontational and disruptive tactics, manifesting in color-coded politics that turned violent and made Thai politics extremely volatile. The era witnessed active yet highly polarized political participation by members of various social classes with opposing ideologies and aligned with different political parties. Frequent regime changes and street violence were the result. With the royal-military elites facing a significant threat from a party supported by grassroots movements, these elites employed various tools to maintain their hold on power, including repression, manipulation of democratic processes, legal coercion, and the co-optation of opposition forces. While these actions subdued their opponents, they were not entirely successful at eliminating a new and formidable grassroots challenge that seriously threatened their power and status.

The 2006 Coup and Its Aftermath: Militarization and Ideological Struggle

His landslide 2005 election victory and subsequent single-party government gave Thaksin political confidence, but generated fear and perturbation among his opponents. Since 2001, Thaksin and his party had succeeded in undermining rival political parties' power bases and provincial politicians' territorial power. But Thaksin had not been able to subvert the main extra-parliamentary force in the Thai polity: the alliance between royalist networks and the military.

Soon after the 2005 election, those opposing Thaksin (business rivals and personal foes, some NGO activists, journalists, academics, and professionals, bureaucrats, and the urban middle class) joined forces against his government. By early 2006, Thaksin's legitimacy was eroded by his controversial business dealings.[13] An anti-government movement led by media mogul Sondhi Limthongkul and Major General Chamlong Srimuang gained momentum. In an attempt to revitalize his legitimacy, the embattled prime minister dissolved parliament and called for a snap election in April 2006. All main opposition parties decided to boycott the election, leaving the TRT party running unopposed. Opposition party leaders claimed that Thaksin had lost legitimacy and the snap election was an attempt to divert public attention from his business scandal. The sudden dissolution of parliament, they argued, also left opposition parties no time to prepare for an election campaign. After the release of the election results, showing that the TRT party won 460 of the 500 seats, anti-Thaksin leaders declared that they rejected the results and would go on rallying until Thaksin resigned and the king appointed a prime minister. The political situation reached an impasse.

Unexpectedly, on April 25, 2006, the king gave a speech to senior judges from the Administrative and Supreme Courts, questioning the democratic

[13] In January 2006, Thaksin's family sold its shares in Shin Corporation, a big telecommunications company, to Temasek Holdings of Singapore for US$1.88 billion. His family gained an enormous profit from this deal and paid no tax, which was legal under Thai law. Their alleged "tax evasion," however, sparked a series of angry demonstrations in Bangkok.

nature of the April general election. He commented that dissolving parliament and calling a snap election (within thirty days) might not have been correct. At the end of his speeches, the king called on the judges and those from the Constitutional Court to work together to resolve the current political crisis (*Matichon*, April 26, 2006). These speeches obviously constituted royal intervention in the midst of the crisis. Two weeks later, the Constitutional Court nullified the April 2006 election and ordered a new election.[14] The Thaksin cabinet decided to hold it on October 15, 2006. This scheduled election never took place.

On September 19, 2006, a group of army leaders staged a coup, the first in fifteen years. The coup leaders extended an invitation to Surayud Chulanont, a former army chief and then privy councilor who had conflicts with Thaksin, to assume the role of prime minister. The timing of the coup was significant; it occurred a month before the proposed election. The coup makers clearly wanted to halt the electoral process. It was the first time in Thai history that a coup was carried out with the intention of directly interfering in the electoral process (previous coups were either conducted to settle conflicts among rival factions within the army or to unseat the government). The post-1997 style of electoral politics had become a major threat to the royal-military alliance. The alliance could not beat Thaksin and his political machine in an election. Its members instead changed the mode of the game by using force. The consequences of the coup were drastic. From 2006–2011, political contestation moved from the electoral arena to the streets, and state and street violence surged (Prajak 2019c).

Many pundits and coup-supporters praised the 2006 coup for its bloodless nature. As political events unfolded, however, it was clear that this coup was the most violent in Thai history, in terms of its subsequent implications. The coup led to a large number of deaths and injuries as it exacerbated conflict, deepened political polarization, and created widespread confrontation between security forces and demonstrators, and among opposing groups of protestors. In the period that followed, Thailand witnessed the emergence of many different forms of violence: the growth of militant social movements (the Yellow Shirts, who were pro-royal/military, and the Red Shirts, who were pro-Thaksin); the use of gangs and thugs in political confrontations; the involvement of paramilitary forces in protests; violent clashes between protesters affiliated with different movements; the resurgence of the politicized army and its violent suppression of citizens; the selective use of force by security groups in dealing with protesters; the use of snipers by the army to kill

[14] The Constitutional Court based its ruling on a technical problem with the voting process, saying that the position of vote booths violated voters' privacy (*Matichon*, May 8, 2006).

protesters; the assassination of mass movement leaders in broad daylight under an emergency decree; assassination attempts and intimidation of privy council members, prime ministers, judges, and election commissioners; bombings in the capital targeting government buildings and protest sites; widespread use of weapons of war on all sides of conflict; and conflict among state security officers.

Apart from resorting to violence, Thaksin's opponents had tried legal avenues to undermine Thaksin's political networks. On May 30, 2007, the Constitutional Court delivered a ruling dissolving the Thai Rak Thai Party and banning 111 party executives from any involvement in political affairs for five years. The judges found some TRT party executives guilty of violating electoral laws in the April 2006 election.[15] TRT members created a new party called Palang Prachachon (People's Power Party, PPP), led by veteran politician Samak Sundaravej, to stand in the 2007 election. Running on a populist policy platform and drawing on Thaksin's popularity, the PPP was victorious and formed a coalition government. However, on September 9, 2008, the Constitutional Court delivered a controversial decision disqualifying Samak from the premiership.[16] The majority of the PPP and coalition parties then voted for Somchai Wongsawat, deputy prime minister and Thaksin's brother-in-law, to be the new premier. Somchai stayed in power for only three months and was forced to step down amidst an occupation by Yellow Shirt protestors of the Bangkok airport, after which the Constitutional Court passed a ruling dissolving the PPP on charges of electoral misconduct, and banning all 109 executive members from politics for five years (*Thai Rath*, December 2, 2007, 1, 16). Immediately after Somchai resigned, military leaders forced some of Thaksin's allies to switch sides and vote for Abhisit Vejjajiva, the leader of the Democrat Party, as the new prime minister.

In the end, these various legal measures failed to undermine Thaksin and his network of support as the Red Shirt movement emerged to support Thaksin's allied parties and oppose the junta-backed government. The Red Shirts were a cross-class political movement of elements of the electorate frustrated at how their elected government had been toppled, their chosen political party dissolved, and their electoral rights abrogated (Keyes 2014; Thanet 2019). In 2009

[15] The court ruled that TRT's leading members had hired certain small parties to run in the April 2006 election to make the election appear competitive and legitimate (*Thai Rath*, May 31, 2007).

[16] According to the court ruling, by performing in a TV cooking show while he was prime minister, Samak acted in breach of the 2007 constitution "prohibiting the Prime Minister and Ministers from having any position in a partnership, a company or an organization carrying out business with a view to sharing profits or incomes or being an employee of any person." The court ruling led to widespread criticism (*Matichon*, September 9, 2008, 1).

and 2010, hundreds of thousands came to Bangkok to ask Abhisit, whose rise to power they deemed illegitimate, to dissolve the House and call a new election. The Abhisit government ordered the army to suppress the protestors who, led by the United Front for Democracy against Dictatorship, were occupying several areas of central Bangkok between April and May 2010. The confrontation between the military and the Red Shirts around the perimeter of the protest site ended up in a violent crackdown on May 19, 2010. At least 90 deaths and over 2,000 injuries occurred, making the April–May clashes the most severe political violence in decades (International Crisis Group 2010; Nostitz 2009).

The locations, methods, perpetrators, and victims of violence in the post-coup era indicate that Thailand was seeing a new pattern of political violence. The army had returned as the main political actor, committing the most violent acts and being responsible for a high proportion of the death toll. The April–May 2010 crackdown represented the most violent political suppression in modern Thai history.[17] The resurgence of state violence after the 2006 coup has been highly detrimental to the progress of democracy as it has worked directly to undermine democratic institutions. State violence of this kind had previously been prevalent during the military dictatorial regimes from the 1950s to 1970s, when state agents had illegitimately acted against political dissidents and enemies (Anderson 1990). During the mid-1980s, however, state violence gradually gave way as the major form to political violence to private killings among politicians and local bosses competing for control over the socioeconomic resources and political positions within a given territory. Candidates' use of violence aimed at winning elections, not disrupting or destroying the electoral process. It was violence in the realm of electoral competition, and, broadly speaking, was respectful to electoral democracy.

When state violence resumed after the 2006 coup, it was largely not directed against individuals, as was the case in the past; rather, it was targeted against broad political forces and institutions that underpinned electoral democracy. This post-2006 coup violence stemmed from the vulnerability of traditional elites and the erosion of their power. Unelected elites thus resorted to violence to reconsolidate their power and undermine their opposition. First of all, the 2006 coup overthrew the popularly elected government and prevented an election. Second, the military-backed Abhisit government (2009–2011) used violence to suppress the electorate's political demands and to derail the electoral process.

[17] Based on official records, seventy-seven people were killed in 1973, forty-three in 1976, and forty-four in 1992. For the protest from March 12 to May 19, 2010, official figures put the death toll at 89 people and about 1,800 others injured. However, the death toll an independent group of academics and NGOs tallied is ninety-four people. See People's Information Center (2012).

The Red Shirt protesters wanted to go to the ballot box to exercise their basic political rights; they were not pursuing armed struggle or trying to overthrow, or even overhaul, the political system. Viewed this way, Abhisit's deployment of tanks and troops (with the tacit support of royalist elites) to suppress the demonstrators had two goals: to silence the voice of urban and rural voters and to delay the re-establishment of electoral democracy. Collusion between the civilian administration of Abhisit and the royal-military elites departed from previous patterns of repression in other ways, too. A civilian government authorized and carried out the crackdown, and it was able to maintain power even after committing mass murders. In 1973 and 1992, crackdowns had been carried out by military-dominated governments. Military prime ministers in both periods had to step down from power after the bloodshed. The 1976 massacre, too, was undertaken by an army faction (with the support of right-wing forces) and constituted a pretext for the army to topple the then-civilian government. In the post-2006 coup era, the royal-military alliance and the Democrat Party had become indispensable political partners and were thus able to resist pressure for accountability.

What made the latest episode of political violence more complex and worrying was the use of coercive force by social movements. Both the Yellow and Red Shirts rhetorically vowed commitment to non-violent struggle, but some of their actual practices violated the principles of non-violence. One of the (notorious) novelties of both movements was the use of hired thugs and gangsters, organized in paramilitary units, to take care of security at protests and other events. These units also worked as security guards for the movements and their top leaders. Many were retired or active uniformed men who had military training. The mobilization styles of both movements were also provocative and confrontational. While most of the Yellow and Red Shirt protesters were unarmed and committed to non-violent practices, the presence of armed elements within them weakened the legitimacy of these movements and made them prone to militarism and violent clashes (International Crisis Group 2010; Nostitz 2009). Overall, the resulting intensified extra-parliamentary conflict in the forms of violent interactions between the opposing movements and the state overwhelmed the country's political life and weakened parliamentary democratic processes.

During 2006–2011, the three most formidable forces in Thai politics were the two color-coded mass political movements and the army. Politicians and political parties were marginal to this new era of street politics. Army interference, judicial activism, and street politics had weakened the parliament and electoral democracy. An unelected elite minority had asserted extra-constitutional power over the political system (Mérieau 2016; Thongchai 2008). With the frequent dissolution of political parties, the truncation of political space, and the deprivation of voting rights, frustrated elements of the electorate had no other option but to engage in mass mobilization. Fundamentally, the eruption of street violence was a by-product of the royal-army alliance's interference in electoral politics. Violent clashes between social movements and the military forces led Thai society deeper into an impasse.

The struggle between the establishment and those aligned with ousted Prime Minister Thaksin during those years deeply transformed Thai politics. Overall, it made political struggle more ideological. Electoral competition is no longer to be dominated by particularistic campaigns but, instead, infused with ideological debate. Voters began to develop different political stances and ideas regarding democratic values, considering issues such as the rule of law, the constitution, judicial activism, and court decisions, and questioning the nature of Thaksin's rule, the role of the military, and the legitimacy of the coup and royal-army political interference. These differing values and ideas affected voting. Color-coded politics and ideological struggle at the national level began to override personal conflict among political bosses and families at the local level.

From the July 2011 to February 2014 Elections: The Changing Terrain of Conflict

Political life in Thailand had a brief moment of calmness in the wake of the 2011 elections, when elections went smoothly and the conflicting parties accepted the results. The glimpse of hope shared among the observers that the conflict-ridden country could seek a (peaceful) way out was terminated by a failed election in February 2014 and another military coup on May 22, 2014.

After almost three years in power, on March 11, 2011, Prime Minister Abhisit dissolved parliament and called for a general election in July. Abhisit seemingly believed that going to the polls early would advantage his party and coalition partners as they had recently passed an annual budget and still controlled the state apparatus. However, ideological politics shaped voting behavior and the conduct of the polls. The 2011 election was dominated by the ideological battle between the anti- and pro-Thaksin movements. In the provinces where the Yellow Shirts or Red Shirts were strong, their members actively volunteered to assist campaigns of parties and candidates that aligned with their movement, replacing the old money-driven, entrepreneurial vote canvassers as key election mobilizers. However, the most crucial factor contributing to the relatively peaceful elections in 2011 was the decision all parties made to play by the electoral rules. The Democrat Party leaders did not boycott the election as they were confident they could win. The Pheu Thai Party, led by Thaksin's sister

Yingluck Shinawatra, was also confident, and conducted a campaign focused on populist policies and political reconciliation.

The Yellow Shirt and Red Shirt movements also refrained from unruly tactics during the campaign. The Yellow Shirts conducted a "Vote-No" campaign, asking voters not to cast ballots for any party, whereas the Red Shirts were aware that any disturbance could provide the army with justification to intervene. Therefore, street violence, which had dominated Thai politics for several years after 2006, did not spill over into the electoral arena. Pheu Thai and Democrat candidates were able to campaign in their opponents' territories safely without opposition supporters interrupting them. With these favorable conditions, the election went smoothly and the victory of the Pheu Thai Party was accepted by their opponents. No violent protest occurred after the poll (Prajak 2016b).

These conditions had disappeared by the time of the February 2014 election. In late December 2013, having faced massive street protests over a controversial amnesty bill, the government of Prime Minister Yingluck Shinawatra dissolved parliament and called for a general election on February 2, 2014.[18] The snap 2014 election witnessed a new pattern of violent conflict: mob violence aimed at disrupting electoral processes and institutions. The protesters were mostly members of the urban middle class and were mobilized by the movement called the People's Democratic Reform Committee (PDRC) led by then deputy head of the Democrat Party, Suthep Thaugsuban. They employed violent tactics to disrupt voter registration, vote casting, and vote counting. As a result, six million registered voters were affected by polling station closure. Eventually, on March 21, 2014, the Constitutional Court ruled February's general election invalid.

The mobilizational strategies and ideological thinking of the PDRC were distinctive. This group received support from a diffuse network of royalist, conservative elite actors, including old wealth, aristocrats, technocrats, presidents of university councils, judges, civil-society leaders, and some business class elites, who saw the Shinawatras and their party machine as a threat. Resources and protection from the traditional elite made it possible for the PDRC to continue their street protest for several months, enabling them to paralyze the government. In terms of mobilization, the PDRC gained support

[18] This controversial amnesty bill pardoned not only ordinary protestors but also protest movement leaders, government leaders who ordered a crackdown on protestors, army leaders and Thaksin, covering the period from 2004 to 2013. This was effectively a "blanket amnesty" for all sides going back to 2004 (excluding crimes of violating Article 112 of the Criminal Code or lèse majesté). The bill passed quite suddenly on November 1, 2014, which led to widespread opposition (Prajak 2016b).

from the urban middle class in Bangkok and from southerners, who were long-standing supporters of the Democrat Party. The movement employed violent, disruptive, and confrontational tactics to destabilize the government, recruiting hired guards, thugs, and state security officers to engage in violent provocations and confrontations with their Red Shirt opponents (Aim 2021; Kanokrat 2021a; Prajak 2016b).

The ideological discourse of the PDRC was ultra-royalist and opposed to electoral democracy. They strongly endorsed official Thai nationalist ideas, centered on the principles of Nation, Religion, and King. They rejected the legitimacy of elections as a means to decide who should govern. Their core belief was that Thai society should be governed by a small group of highly educated, moralistic, self-proclaimed "good people," through royal appointment, instead of by "bad politicians" elected by the majority of voters who were still poor and uneducated. The movement's leaders declared they wanted to establish the movement itself as the sovereign and "reform" the country through a non-elected "People's Council." Their main slogan was "reform before elections" and they presented themselves as righteous and patriotic actors who desired to "cleanse" Thai society of corrupt politicians and stem the influence of ignorant rural masses. Suthep outlined plans for the People's Council to act as a legislative body, amend laws, and carry out a reform plan. The council would include 400 members, 300 of whom would represent various occupations, while the PDRC would select the rest. According to the PDRC plan, the country would be "frozen" for two years without elections while their "reform" process was undertaken. The PDRC demanded Yingluck's immediate resignation in order to pave way for a new government led by an unelected prime minister (Prajak 2016b).

The PDRC was the first major social movement in Thai political history that directly attacked electoral processes and institutions. They condemned not only parties and politicians but also the democratic system as a whole. Thailand had previously witnessed political movements that protested against certain government policies, or that condemned corrupt parties and politicians, but had none that explicitly protested against the democratic system itself. Even the People's Alliance for Democracy (PAD), which was the predecessor to and twin of the PDRC, had not rejected elections and the entire democratic system. The PDRC, unlike the PAD, did not accept that elections could be a mechanism for resolving political conflict and deciding who should govern the country. Its leaders rejected wholeheartedly the basic principle of "one person, one vote" and that all Thai citizens should have equal political rights. Instead of conducting a "Vote-No" campaign, the PDRC did everything it could to prevent elections from happening. The PDRC's ultra-royalist ideology and animosity toward elections marked an unprecedented development in the country's prolonged political conflict, making starkly explicit the essential ideological conflict between royalism and popular democracy (see Aim 2021; Kanokrat 2021a; Janjira 2020). The PDRC's street protests effectively created a state of anarchy and political paralysis, which paved the way for another military takeover when, in May 2014, the head of the army, General Prayut Chan-ocha, staged a coup which toppled the Yingluck government, ushering in a new phase of repressive military rule.

Overall, Thailand has been a deeply polarized and unstable country for almost two decades. Since 2005, the country that was once a champion of democracy in ASEAN has been engulfed by recurrent large-scale street violence and deeply divided between supporters of opposing mass movements. It has become a site of chronic political instability, state paralysis, democratic breakdown, and growing authoritarianism. There has been no consensus around basic rules of the game among conflicting elites and mass movements. During 2005–2014, Thailand had seven prime ministers (five elected, two unelected and installed by military coup), five general elections (and two nullified elections), two military coups, and four large-scale violent suppressions of public protests. Two popularly elected prime ministers were ousted by military coups, two others by court rulings. From 2014 to 2019, Thailand was the only country globally being governed under direct military rule. The coup-installed government led by General Prayut was the longest-serving military authoritarian government the country had witnessed since the 1950s (Prajak and Veerayooth 2018).

The military coups of both 2006 and 2014, instead of solving the predicament, further exacerbated political divisions. The latest coup in 2014 did not resolve political and social division; instead, the military tried to suppress division with coercive force and draconian laws. As a result, the country remains afflicted by civil strife and is far from reaching a new political arrangement all sides perceive as legitimate. The 2017 constitution, designed to prolong the power of the junta, has deepened confrontation between opposing political forces as it establishes a political system that maintains the dominance of the royal-military power bloc and unelected elites at the expense of civilian politicians and civil-society groups.

The Interlinkage between Intra-elite Power Struggle and Mass-based Conflict

What is the best theoretical framework to explain the volatile political crisis witnessed in Thailand since the rise of Thaksin and his populist party? This section offers a synthesized analytical framework that can best explain the crisis of democracy in Thai society. Since the crisis started, scholars of Thai politics have debated how to understand it. The debate is divided into two camps: those who view the conflict as a typical elite power struggle of a type frequently witnessed in Thailand since the 1932 revolution, and those who see it as a revolt of the downtrodden.

Those who propose that the crisis is centered on elite contestation argue that the civil-society organizations and protesters on the streets are tools used by elites from both sides as they prosecute their political battles (see Montesano, Pavin, and Aekapol 2012 and Apichart et al. 2013). However, this "elite struggle" framework has several shortcomings. By reducing supporters of both sides to pawns of rival elites, it fails to explain the autonomous roles played by ordinary people. At times, such roles have been important. One clear example of where elite and mass preferences diverged was the response to the decision of Yingluck Shinawatra's government to pass a bill providing blanket amnesty to all conflicting parties; many Red Shirt supporters fiercely opposed this bill (Thaweeporn 2013).

While the "mass revolt" approach fails to account sufficiently for the extent to which contending elites have initiated and shaped the conflict, the "elite struggle" theory also fails to explain the intensity of social division among Thai people, which goes far beyond the elite's agenda and control. Thaksin and his elite rivals were prime movers of polarized conflict, but they did not dictate the entire direction and dynamics of conflict. If polarization in Thailand were merely a matter of elite contestation, it would not have lasted for more than a decade: One side would have won the political fight, or both sides would have ended up with a political deal. It was so protracted precisely because so many ordinary people were drawn into conflict: Thaksin's policies and actions helped activate key social cleavages (regional cleavages, urban–rural divide, and class divisions) that existed in Thai society long before he came to power. His policies, such as the village fund, debt moratorium, and universal health care, empowered lower and lower middle class people in rural areas and made urban middle and upper classes feel threatened and insecure (Ferrara 2015; Walker 2012). The decision by the royal-military network to employ unconstitutional measures to eliminate Thaksin in turn fueled disgruntlement among the lower and middle class people who supported Thaksin. The radicalization of Thaksin and his supporters in defense of electoral democracy, in turn, deepened fear and insecurity within the allied establishment-middle class, which then countered with more aggressive measures, leading to an escalation of conflict.

As these attempts to explain polarization in Thailand suggest, it is rather misleading to argue exclusively for one factor or aspect; instead, we need an integrative framework that combines several factors in a systematic way and allows us to understand the dynamics and evolution of conflict, rather than proposing a static, monocausal model (McCoy, Rahman and Somer 2018). To understand the crisis in Thailand, ones need to understand both elite and mass layers of conflict, and how their interaction has driven polarization. Critically, we need to understand how individual, institutional, structural and ideological factors have shaped this interaction. Let us address each of these briefly in turn.

Elite Factors: Power Struggle and Politics of Insecurity

Thaksin strove to achieve a monopoly of power through electoral politics. Thaksin's campaign was centered primarily on nationalist policies to rescue the business sector and populist policies to help the poor in both rural and urban areas. This strategy proved to be highly popular given the hardship faced by these groups in the post-1997 economic crisis context. In the process, this policy campaign helped drive a political transformation from the old pattern of factional politics to a new pattern of party-dominated, policy-oriented politics led by a populist leader. Thaksin mobilized state resources to address the social grievances and aspirations of the rural electorate, who have, in turn, emerged as a vital social force since the late 1990s (Walker 2012). In purely electoral terms, the rural electorate is highly significant as they account for two-third of votes.

Thaksin, however, was not a left-wing populist in the style of certain Latin American leaders, nor a European-type right-wing populist (Mudde and Kaltwasser 2018; Roberts 2006). Rather, Kasian labeled him as pursuing a "populism for capitalism" (Kasian 2006, 10). In fact, his populism evolved over time. At the beginning, Thaksin did not position his party as populist; it was critics who labeled him and his policies in this way (Yoshifumi 2009). Instead, Thaksin's policies aimed primarily at winning a majority of votes. They also aimed to pacify the masses and prevent social unrest in the context of widespread lower class discontent after the economic crisis of the late 1990s. Only when Thaksin was attacked by the establishment did he employ populist rhetoric and practices to mobilize mass support and challenge established elites. The Red Shirt movement only emerged after the 2006 coup when his opponents ousted Thaksin. Without an organized mass movement, Thaksin realized that his position would be vulnerable. Polarization was therefore fueled by an action-reaction dynamic; it was neither structurally predetermined nor planned by elites.

Why did traditional elites feel threatened by Thaksin? There are both material and psychological explanations. Thaksin's immense popularity and his dominant party indirectly challenged the power, interests, and prestige of the network monarchy (i.e. that broad collection of interests arranged around the monarchy). It challenged the monarchy's "claim to be the sole focus of political loyalty" (Pasuk and Baker 2009, 89), as well as the monarchy's role as supreme political authority and arbiter within the Thai polity. Moreover, with the looming succession crisis (when Thaksin first came to power King Bhumibol was seventy-four years old and showing signs of frailty) and the fact that the crown prince was unpopular and uncharismatic but close to Thaksin, actors within the network monarchy feared that Thaksin would become a kingmaker and assert strong influence over the palace during the next reign (Pavin 2020; Thongchai 2016).

The psychological effects of the looming succession crisis cannot be downplayed. This crisis seemed to cloud the judgment of many within palace circles. The network monarchy is fundamentally a personalized network centered on the monarch, which derived its power from the king's charisma. A change in the network's head figure would thus likely reduce the power of the whole network. And it was not only power and prestige that were at stake. In terms of economic interests, the royal family's Crown Property Bureau (CPB) is one of the largest business conglomerates in Thailand, with assets of approximately US$41 billion in 2005 (Hewison 2012, 149–150; Porphant 2008). The Crown Property Bureau is an opaque organization, exempt from taxes, protected by the palace, and lacking transparency and public accountability (Puangchon 2019). More broadly, since the 1950s, the power of the royal-military alliance had incrementally increased over time, and had never been significantly reduced or reformed, providing alliance members with the capacity to intervene in and destabilize politics when they deemed their interests threatened.

At the same time, Thaksin's authoritarian and illiberal tendencies (Chaiwat 2006; Kasian 2006) worsened the situation, and muddied the lines of cleavage, by pushing away a number of journalists, NGO activists, and academics likely to support democracy, and prompting them to ally with the royal-military elite. These civil-society actors were alienated by Thaksin's divisive rhetoric and practices, including the erosion of democratic institutions under his rule, and his government's human rights violations and suppression of civil liberties (e.g. in his brutal "war on drugs" in which approximately 2,800 people were victims of extrajudicial killings, with over half having no connection to drug dealing or any apparent reason for their deaths (Human Rights Watch 2008)). They disapproved of Thaksin's attempts to undermine checks and balances. While the poor admired Thaksin, seeing him as speaking for them, his critics thought he was becoming increasingly autocratic. They felt that, under Thaksin's government, their political space had shrunk and their influence had disappeared. Eventually, many of these middle class activists chose to support the anti-Thaksin elite in bringing Thaksin down. Unfortunately, the royal-military elite replaced Thaksin's illiberal democracy with their own military authoritarianism in 2006 and 2014, deepening the crisis of democracy in Thailand (Prajak 2019e).

Institutional Factors: Constitutional and Electoral System Design

Constitutional rules and institutional mechanisms also played a part in creating the crisis in two main ways. First, with its goal of strengthening the position of the prime minister and stabilizing government, the 1997 constitution gave enormous power to the prime minister over MPs and his own party members, and made it relatively difficult for the lower house to hold the prime minister accountable. This exacerbated Thaksin's authoritarian tendencies and raised the stakes of opposing him. Second, the disproportional nature of the mixed-member majoritarian (MMM) electoral system gave Thaksin's party a lot of "extra" seats, so that it overwhelmingly dominated the parliament. For example, in the 2001 election, the TRT party gained 37.06 percent of constituency votes and 40.64 percent of party-list votes, but obtained 49.6 percent of seats in parliament (Nelson 2002, Table 8.9).

Another significant factor contributing to the crisis was the main opposition party's inability to reform itself, formulate a credible alternative policy platform, and respect the democratic rules of the game. Despite its long-established presence, the Democrat Party has experienced repeated electoral defeats since the 1995 election, primarily due to its inability to undertake substantial party reform and expand its limited support base. The party mainly positions itself as a party of conservative voters, consisting of the urban middle class in Bangkok and relatively affluent voters in the south, while failing to win support from rural voters in the north and northeast due to its elitist outlook and urban bias. In fact, the regional composition of parliamentary seats in Thailand (in the 2001 and 2005 elections) explains Thaksin's success and his opponents' failure: There were 86 seats in the south and Bangkok, but 193 in the north and northeast. As long as the Democrat Party failed to win support in relatively poor northern and northeastern constituencies, it would be unable to win. Indeed, since Thaksin came to power, the Democrat Party has lost to Thaksin-backed parties in every election the Democrats contested. During the crisis in 2005–2006, the party boycotted the election and decided to side with the Yellow Shirts and network monarchy in toppling Thaksin through extra-parliamentary methods. In 2014, it boycotted the election again. This time it directly led the mass protest which eventually paved the way for the coup that May (Aim 2021; Prajak 2016b).

The judicial and oversight institutions that the 1997 constitution created to function as check-and-balance mechanisms also failed due to their lack of capacity and integrity, unclear jurisdiction and scope of power, and interference by Thaksin and old elites. When Thaksin was dominant, these institutions ruled in favor of Thaksin; when the establishment decided to eliminate him, they switched sides. The Constitutional Court disbanded Thaksin-allied parties twice and banned hundreds of their party members from participating in politics, disqualified two prime ministers from the Thaksin camp, blocked constitutional amendment attempts, and nullified elections in 2006 and 2014, on both occasions producing political deadlock and a military coup. The highly partisan role of these accountability mechanisms, especially the politicization of the judiciary, deepened polarization by undermining the rule of law and removing means of settling conflict peacefully and democratically (Dressel and Khemthong 2019).

Structural and Ideological Factors: Inequality, Political Disenfranchisement, and Competing Ideologies

Beyond these elite and institutional levels of conflict, polarization in Thailand also has deep roots at the structural level. Social and economic inequality and political disenfranchisement generated deep social grievances related to underlying social cleavages based on class, ideology, the urban–rural divide, and regional identity. We cannot single out any one cleavage as *the* critical explanatory factor. Instead, these cleavages are interrelated and reinforce one another in providing conditions for the emergence of both the anti- and pro-Thaksin movements, and for deepening the polarization between them.

As mentioned earlier, polarization in Thailand has involved not only the elite, but also large numbers of ordinary people. At its peak, both the Yellow Shirt and Red Shirt movements could mobilize 200,000–300,000 of their supporters to join their street protests (Nostitz 2014). Several million more supported the movements through media channels each movement owned. The Thaksin-backed party and the Democrat Party attracted 15 and 11 million voters, respectively, in the 2011 election.

Socioeconomic and ideological factors help account for the division between the Yellow and the Red camps, with socioeconomic factors explaining the movements' social origins, and ideology explaining the commitment and enthusiasm of movement participants. Polarization between the two coalitions was broadly based on regional, urban–rural, and class divisions. Voting patterns in elections from 2001 to 2014 show a clear repeated pattern in which Thaksin gained overwhelming support in the north and northeast plus some provinces in central Thailand and the provinces surrounding Bangkok, while the Democrats dominated in the south and among urban districts of Bangkok.

Underlying this stable pattern are social cleavages, with structural inequality a key driver. By 2012, the income gap between the top 20 percent and the bottom 20 percent of the population was approximately thirteen times, compared to four times in Japan and Scandinavia, and six to eight times in North America and Europe (Pasuk and Baker, 2012, 218–219). By 2019, with an income Gini coefficient of 43.3 percent, Thailand had the highest income inequality in East and Southeast Asia (World Bank 2022). In this sense, the crisis manifested in Thailand supports the argument that inequality tends to undermine the stability of democratic regimes, because elites have more to lose from redistributive policies that tend to result from majority rule (Acemoglu and Robinson 2006, 35–37).

In Thailand's north and northeast, where support for Thaksin has been strong, incomes are relatively low and poverty is pronounced. Even though absolute poverty has been declining over time, income disparity has widened. More than 80 percent of the group with the lowest income is concentrated in rural areas in these regions. In 2007, average incomes in the north and northeast were about one-third of those in Bangkok. Provinces that voted for the Democrat Party that year had an average per capita gross provincial product of 221,130 baht per year, contrasted to 92,667 baht for provinces that voted for the Thaksin-backed party (UNDP Report 2009 quoted in Hewison 2012, 156). In addition, a national survey found that people who joined the Red Shirt movement had lower incomes, education, and job/life security (because a majority worked in agriculture and the informal sector) than those who supported the Yellow Shirt movement (Apichart et al. 2013).

Most Red Shirt supporters came from the north and northeast and from the suburbs of Bangkok (where migrant workers from the northeast are concentrated). Core members of the Red Shirt movement were mostly drawn from rural farmers in these poor regions. Though many of them also supplemented their family income with non-farm jobs, they still maintained their peasant, rural identity (Keyes 2014; Walker 2012). Thus, in Thailand, regional cleavages, the urban–rural divide, and class divisions are largely mutually reinforcing.

Once it began, the conflict between the anti- and pro-Thaksin groups made the multiplicity of interests and identities that make up Thai society align along a single dimension, dividing Thais into two opposing political camps separated by a rigid boundary and marked by seemingly zero-sum interests and mutually exclusive identities. Political competition became an existential war of survival, with opponents transformed into enemies to be "eradicated."

But this analysis still begs the question of why, given that underdevelopment of the north and northeast and wealth disparities had been problems for decades, the polarization began when it did. Here, the key explanation is that the underlying condition of inequality was activated politically by several intervening factors in the late 1990s. The critical juncture was 1997, when the country witnessed three developments: the most severe financial crisis in modern Thai history, a new constitution which changed the rules of the political game, and a decentralization program which affected the state structure. The financial crisis made poor people distressed and changed the power balance within the elite. The new constitution provided advantages to whoever could build a large party with a policy-based campaign, an expansive political network, and major resources. Decentralization empowered local constituencies and made them aware of the power of the ballot. Frequent local elections strengthened electoral democracy at the grassroots level and undermined the power of the old bureaucratic machine (Viengrat 2019).

Prior to 1997, almost no political parties offered concrete policies to voters. Instead, they were built around small networks of business or bureaucratic cadres and lacked clear ideological platforms. Weak coalitions meant elected governments failed to last long enough to implement significant policies or be responsive to voters. The Thaksin party's populist package and strong government changed Thai politics, not only making democracy work but also making it "edible" (the Red Shirt term) in the views of members of the marginalized electorate. Under Thaksin, these voters felt empowered and began to aspire for better opportunities in life: education for their children, cheap health care for the elderly, micro-credits for their small businesses, and so on. When Thaksin was ousted unconstitutionally, they felt not only that "their dear leader" was brought down illegitimately, but also that their life progress was being halted by the establishment and urban elites. In short, unfulfilled political and social desires underpinned the political mobilization of the Red Shirts (Sopranzetti 2012).

The Red Shirt movement was thus neither an anti-capitalist movement nor revolutionary. It demanded basic equal political rights under electoral democracy, a responsive government, and wider opportunities for social mobility. Red Shirts viewed the policy packages of Thaksin as attempts to promote redistribution and to reduce the negative effects that the capital-wielding urban elites had on the social mobility of rural and urban working class citizens (Glassman 2010; Sopranzetti 2018).

On the other side of the political division, the urban middle class opposed Thaksin as they found Thaksin's rhetoric and practices repugnant and irresponsible. They also felt that they were the ones bearing the cost (through their income taxes) of Thaksin's programs that benefited the lower class much more than them. They feared that their living standards and status would cease to improve or even deteriorate (Ferrara 2015, 273).

In Thailand, urban middle class citizens are influential in shaping public opinion and social agendas, but in electoral politics they are a minority, greatly outnumbered by rural voters. This situation made the urban middle class feel powerless. When Thaksin cemented virtually unassailable support among rural voters in a way no politician had done before, the urban middle class eventually turned against not only Thaksin, but against electoral democracy itself. In 2014, many of them actively joined the PDRC-led protest to disrupt the voting process and publicly stated that the basic principle of "one person, one vote" was not suitable for Thailand, because most voters were still poor, uneducated, and ignorant. This attitude drew on long-standing cultural biases among middle class urbanites against rural people. What was new was how urban elites appropriated this cultural prejudice to legitimize their political campaign to deprive rural people of their political rights (Aim 2021; Prajak 2016b).

Nevertheless, it should be noted that the rise of Thaksin did not change the attitudes of the middle class immediately. In 2001 and 2005, TRT still won the majority of seats in Bangkok. Middle class opposition toward Thaksin developed over time and was shaped by Thaksin's own self-aggrandizing approach and by the traditional elite's maneuvers to sideline him. Therefore, both underlying structural factors *and* framing of conflict came into play in shaping people's attitudes and behaviors in ways that led to polarization. Royalist elites and anti-Thaksin media were "effective in arousing the insecurities and fears of urban middle class voters, warning that Thaksin's populism would come at the expense of their economic well-being and social status" (Ferrara 2015, 257).[19]

The changing media landscape helped fuel the political tension. The anti-Thaksin camp used social media and satellite TV (owned directly by Yellow Shirt leader Sondhi Limthongkul) to spread rumors and disinformation directed against Thaksin and his supporters. Later, the Red Shirts copied the same tactics, having their own TV stations and radio channels which propagated opposing narratives to counter the Yellow Shirts' media. The media space itself thus became a site of fierce political battle and was flooded with hate speech and malign messages rather than informed public deliberation. Demonization and dehumanizing discourses were pervasive. Yellow Shirts called the Red Shirts "buffalos," "lizards," and "scum of the earth," while the Red Shirts labeled the Democrat Party the "cockroach party." One observer highlighted "the increasing segmentation of information markets" in Thai society, which provided "little scope for negotiating principled political differences" (Unger 2012, 321). People in opposing camps experienced different political realities,

[19] Elite manipulation of the media and inflaming of public feelings have played a role in democratic breakdown in many countries; see Haggard and Kaufman (2021).

consuming different news, and living in two different political worlds. Later, under the post-2014 military regime, Thailand saw incessant cyber policing, cyber witch-hunts, and mass propaganda promoted by the state-controlled media, further exacerbating social conflict (Pinkaew 2016; Schaffar 2016).

In summary, while the class structure and regional and urban–rural disparities provided the conditions for mass mobilization and resulting polarization, it was elite conflict that activated these cleavages. Elite ideological framing exacerbated and deepened polarization even as it spiraled out of elites' control. Over time, the protagonists came to frame and perceive political conflict as uncompromising political warfare between the "good" and the "bad," the "moral, clean, enlightened" and the "immoral, corrupt, stupid," the "patriots" and the "traitors," and the "aristocrats" and the "commoners." Political entrepreneurs on both sides produced this divisive discourse, and the gulf between their political goals widened. The Yellow Shirts and traditional elites wanted to restore "Thai-style democracy" (i.e. despotic paternalism or elitist democracy) based on royal nationalism and a hierarchical social order that drew on traditional cultural values. In contrast, the Red Shirts espoused support for a "populist democracy" with a strong elected government, underpinned by popular nationalism and an egalitarian social order founded on a basic principle of political equality (Keyes 2012; Naruemon 2016).

In sum, from the 2006 coup to the time of the Yingluck government and the PDRC protests, lack of consensus around the basic rules of the political game among key power elites and key civil-society groups generated intense political conflict. The relatively stable pre-1997 political order, in which the provincial elites, national capitalists, and royal-military leaders shared power under a weak parliamentary system, has long collapsed and is unlikely to be revived. However, the 2006 coup derailed the emerging post-1997 order that arose from an economic crisis and a new constitution and paved the way for a strong prime minister and a responsive electoral democracy. After that, the country was torn apart by civil strife and political violence, with the conflicting groups unable to agree on a new political order. As time passed, the looming royal succession intensified the fear and insecurity of members of the royal-military alliance, who worried that the post-Bhumibol era would be unstable and detrimental to their power and status (Pavin 2020). Against this backdrop, the army staged the 2014 coup to ensure an orderly and peaceful royal succession.

5 The Struggle for (New) Political Order (2014–Present)

On May 22, 2014, a new military junta, using the name of the National Council for Peace and Order (NCPO), led by General Prayut Chan-ocha, came to power after staging a coup that toppled the elected government of Yingluck Shinawatra, sister of former prime minister Thaksin Shinawatra. The coup-installed assembly appointed Prayut to serve as the country's new prime minister. Prayut brought back a form of rule in which the military dominated Thai politics under the auspices of the monarchy. His military-controlled government promised to return democracy to Thailand after it had implemented "reform" programs. In the meantime, it restricted civil liberties, curtailed free speech, prosecuted critics, and prohibited political activity. Meanwhile, generals established themselves as the new ruling elite, enhancing their own status, scope of power, budgets, and manpower. They also planned to maintain their dominance through constitutional design by weakening majoritarian democracy and undermining the influence of political parties and civil society (Prajak 2016a).

The 2014 coup, orchestrated by General Prayut, and the transition to a new reign in 2016, following the passing of King Bhumibol, marked the onset of a new era in Thai politics. The political situation appeared calm on the surface, but Thai society remained as deeply polarized as ever; the coup did not transform ideological conflicts, but it merely suppressed them with brute force. However, the regime's characteristics underwent significant changes, the state ideology centered on the hegemony of the monarchy faced challenges, and the network monarchy entered a state of critical transition. In this shifting landscape, royal-military elites strove to maintain their power by doubling down. Prayut sought to resurrect a despotic paternalistic style of rule that was reminiscent of Sarit's, emplacing it within a semi-democratic setting like that under Prem.

While democratic backsliding continued during Prayut's prolonged tenure, backed by the military and the palace, the pro-democracy movement countered by mobilizing extra-parliamentary politics and challenging Prayut in electoral contests. A new pro-democracy coalition was coming into being. Highly contentious elections in both 2019 and 2023 revealed new voting patterns and political aspirations, indicating the commencement of a new phase of struggle to establish a redefined political order under the evolving power of the monarchy.

Designing Institutions to Prolong Authoritarianism: The 2014 Coup and Its Constitutional Design

Worldwide, since the end of the Cold War, military coups and military governments have gradually become anachronistic. Only a few poverty-stricken countries still experience political intervention by the army or military coups (Bermeo 2016). Military regimes have fallen out of fashion. Among countries which have experienced a post–Cold War successful military coup, Thailand is the most economically developed. The fact that direct military coups toppled elected governments twice in less than a decade in such a relatively developed country is a clear sign of the unusually high levels of political instability in Thailand.[20]

Fundamentally, the NCPO's May 2014 coup was a continuation of the previous coup that occurred in September 2006. In 2006, coup leaders had merely slightly changed the constitution, and so had failed to prevent Thaksin and his network from coming back to power. The generals responsible for the 2014 coup learned from that failure and thus intended to write completely new rules of the game with the goal of dismantling Thaksin's power and reshaping democracy. After the coup, the junta appointed a tiny and conservative committee to draft a new constitution, resulting in the controversial 2017 constitution. Fundamentally, this constitution represented the latest effort by the Thai establishment to maintain their political power under the guise of constitutional rule (Siripan 2018).

To understand the coup leaders' political thinking, one needs to take Thailand's socio-political context from 2006 to 2014 into account. In 2014, the military intervened fundamentally to protect the power and interests of the royal-military elites because of what they saw as three main threats to the old hierarchical political order. First and foremost was the looming royal succession and its unknown consequences, which traditional elites feared might affect their privileges and power. Succession made the establishment highly anxious (Pavin 2020). Second, was the persistently solid mass-based support among the rural and urban poor for the Thaksin camp, which had won repeated landslide ballot victories since 2001, winning power through a process in which the military had little skill or influence. Last, were the color-coded street politics that had arisen since the last coup and were generating persistent violent extra-parliamentary activism by opposing mass movements. These three factors pressed the military to act to reassert its own influence. Per this view, royal-military elites staged the 2014 coup out of fear and anxiety, not confidence (Prajak 2019a).

Against this backdrop, the army felt it was necessary for it to control the "transition period," (i.e. the period of royal succession). Army leaders feared there would be a power vacuum at a moment of political fragility. They believed that only their institution could guarantee the stability of the system of royal-military dominance, and that doing this required suppressing the political parties and people's movements and controlling parliamentary democracy.

[20] For data on the changing pattern of coups in the post–Cold War era, see Derpanopoulos, Frantz, Geddes, and Wright (2016) and Marinov and Goemans (2014).

The military's political strategy was to reorder the political structure in ways that would keep the power of traditional elites intact. Yet coup leaders were also aware of the illegitimacy of direct military rule in the post–Cold War era and therefore, in the long term, saw they would need to sustain power by maintaining a façade of democracy to gain legitimacy from citizens and the international community.

The junta, led by General Prayut and General Pravit Wongsuwan, thus set about to restructure the political system. They re-centralized the state structure by enhancing the duties and scope of power of the military at the expense of civil society and elected local administrations. They also took steps to curb majoritarian democracy by weakening political parties. The 2017 constitution established a bicameral National Assembly, consisting of an elected House of Representatives (with 500 members) and an appointed Senate (with 250 members). The lower house's term was four years, while the Senate's was five years. In the first five years, the NCPO had the authority to appoint the members of the Senate, with six seats reserved for the security forces.[21] The NCPO leaders claimed that incorporating the security forces into the Senate would prevent future military coups. The Senate also had the power to select the premier, along with the lower house, a provision designed to ensure that Prayut could return to power after the elections.

Apart from the appointed Senate, the 2017 constitution empowered independent watchdog organizations (the election commission, anti-corruption commission, Constitutional Court, etc.) which can function as veto mechanisms that can check and disqualify the elected government. Since 2006, these organizations had already been actors powerful enough to paralyze or unseat popularly elected administrations. Several times, their decisions, especially the Constitutional Court's rulings, have effectively changed the balance of power (Dressel and Khemthong 2019; Mérieau 2016).

Another institutional mechanism created to weaken majoritarian democracy under the 2017 constitution is the newly designed electoral system. The electoral system was changed from an MMM system to a so-called mixed-member apportionment (MMA) system. Under the MMA system, there are 350 constituency seats and 150 party-list seats. Instead of casting two separate votes (one for a candidate and one for a party list), under the new system, voters cast only one vote, which counts simultaneously as both a vote for the chosen candidate and for that candidate's party, in calculating party-list seats. Any party's total share of seats is determined by the total number of votes that party receives

[21] After five years, the senate would be selected by an electorate composed of nominated professional groups.

nationwide via the constituency vote. The purpose is to fragment the Thai party system and make it difficult for any party to win a clear majority, with the goal of weakening Thaksin-aligned parties (Prajak and Veerayooth 2018).

Fundamentally, the 2017 constitution was designed to strengthen the power of unelected elite institutions: the monarchy, the army, the judiciary, and independent organizations. It made it easier for these institutions to disqualify any elected government and its leaders if they lacked traditional elite support. It also empowered the various independent organizations to monitor and constrain the government's use of the budget. It thus greatly reduced the autonomy of the elected government. In short, military elites had designed new rules of the game through which they believed they could control the country without resorting to a military coup. The regime created by the 2017 constitution could thus be characterized as a form of military-guided semi-authoritarianism. Through institutional design, military elites tried to tame majoritarian democracy and make it difficult for Thaksin and his network to return to power.

The Entrenchment of Military Power: Institution, Nepotism, and Co-optation

Although the 2014 coup was a continuation of the 2006 coup, the power structure and governing rules the 2014 coup leaders used were new. In the 2014 coup, army leaders established direct military rule, centralizing power and decision-making processes in the military institution and among junta leaders. The coup regime of General Prayut was divided into five organs: the NCPO, Cabinet, National Legislative Assembly (NLA), National Reform Council (NRC), and Constitution Drafting Committee. It was clear from the composition of each organ that the military dominated the power structure.

First and foremost, the NCPO, as the most powerful organization after the coup, was completely controlled by the junta. Coup leader Prayut made himself prime minister instead of giving the position to a non-military leader, like in the 2006 coup. Military leaders controlled all key ministries related to national security, including defense and the interior. They also stepped in to control other ministries that went beyond their knowledge and expertise, including the ministries of foreign affairs, transport, agriculture and cooperatives, natural resources and environment, energy, commerce, labor, justice, and education (though later, due to apparent incompetence under the military cabinet members in charge of these ministries, the NCPO had to replace them with more capable civilians). The Prayut cabinet was predominantly a military cabinet. Compared to the coup-installed government of General Surayud Chulanont (2006–2007), one can clearly see the stark difference. Surayud was not among the coup leaders but was appointed because of his position as a privy councilor trusted by the king. Besides Surayud, his whole cabinet had only two military figures in charge of ministries; after the 2014 coup, there were twelve military cabinet ministers. If the 2006 coup was a coup of royalists carried out by the army, the 2014 coup was a coup of the army by the army (Prajak and Veerayooth 2018).

In 2006, the junta leaders (who ruled for only fifteen months) appointed sixty-five military personnel to serve in the 242-member coup-installed NLA, accounting for 26 percent of the Assembly. After the 2014 coup, the figure rose to 58 percent. Interestingly, Prayut appointed every chief of the army, navy, and air force since 2007 to the NLA. This reflected an attempt by the NCPO to base its rule on a broad institutional core within the armed forces. However, it should be noted that nepotism was also present in the Prayut regime. Prayut appointed thirty-six of his former subordinates, seventeen of his classmates, and his own younger brother to positions in the NLA. Prawit Wongsuwan, another key NCPO leader and defense minister, appointed two of his younger brothers to the NLA. Even so, the broad institutional support base of the regime within the armed forces helps explain the relative longevity and success of the NCPO (Prajak and Veerayooth 2018).

The NRC comprised 250 members and was appointed to formulate a "reform proposal" for the country. Compared to the NLA, the NRC had little actual power, but the NCPO used it as a platform to co-opt and reward civilian members of the coup coalition, notably leaders of civil and political society who had been involved in the anti-Thaksin movement and had thus helped pave the way for the coup. The NRC's members included active and retired public servants, prominent academics, wealthy businesspersons, high-profile senators, Yellow Shirt leaders, leading NGO activists and journalists, and politicians from several parties.

Through the NRC and other newly founded committees and sub-committees, the junta played the politics of co-optation by providing coalition supporters – and potential opponents – with public positions, financial benefits, and a formal space to voice their demands. The NCPO made those selected feel that, at least, they had some access to power under the military-controlled regime. Though some of the technocrats, academics, journalists, and NGO activists involved were skeptical of the NCPO, they were also pragmatists and took the opportunity to push forward their policy agendas and voice their grievances. In effect, however, they helped protect and sustain military rule. By successfully co-opting various groups of people, the NCPO developed a support base in political and civil society (Somchai 2020; Veerayooth 2016).

In the new era of transition after the royal succession in October 2016, the royal-military elite began a new period of uncertainty. The long-established political order had been centered on a charismatic and popular monarch, loyally served by the army. This system could no longer properly function without the late King Bhumibol Adulyadej, while a replacement political order in the subsequent era has not yet clearly emerged. The military leadership did not want a power vacuum to occur in this fragile time and strongly believed that only the army could ensure an orderly and peaceful transition. They also aspired to control the direction of the transition. Thus, the military, as the core of the old governing elite in Thailand, stepped in during the period of royal succession to effectively take direct control of the distribution of power and interests in the new reign (Prajak and Veerayooth 2018).

After the 2014 coup, the military effectively sought to place itself in the position of a hegemonic ruler. This was evident in various fields. The budget provided for increased military privileges, salaries, and troops. Military personnel were placed in charge of state enterprises and state, as well as independent organizations. The military's power was enshrined within the constitution. For example, after the coup, military generals maneuvered to control lucrative state-owned enterprises (SOEs). In 2017, forty SOEs had military personnel as their board members, which was a 100 percent increase from the pre-coup era, and sixteen enterprises had military generals as their board presidents, a fivefold increase from the civilian administration before the coup (BBC Thai 2017).[22] Most importantly, by having the 250 senators (equivalent to half of the lower house) directly appointed by the NCPO, the military practically became the largest political party in the new political system, with the power to nominate and select its own prime minister (Prajak 2016a).

Depoliticising Society: Suppression and Demobilization

Another key characteristic of the Prayut regime was its attempt to manage dissent and depoliticize society. In the foregoing section, we discussed the regime's co-optation of civil-society groups into the coup coalition led by the junta. However, not every civil-society group was co-opted.

After the coup, a group of progressive Red Shirt activists, academics, and student leaders remained critical of military rule and protested against the regime. The Prayut administration perceived these anti-coup dissidents as a potential source of destabilization who thus needed to be marginalized and silenced through intimidation and repression. Given the small number of anti-coup activists, the NCPO initially pursued a strategy of targeted repression instead of widespread coercion. It detained a large number of dissidents in

[22] For the historical development of the relationship between military wealth and coups in Thailand, see Kanda (2021) and Ukrist and Connors (2019).

military camps, forced them to go through "attitude adjustment programs" (i.e. intimidation and psychological torture), arbitrarily visited their houses and workplaces and took them for interrogation, and charged them with various draconian laws entailing severe punishment (Haberkorn 2014; Puangthong 2021).

The ultimate aim of these repressive measures was not taking lives but creating fear and silence, making targeted dissidents fearful of making public comments or mobilizing mass protests. Given that the government's bureaucratic machine was itself divided and weak, the Prayut regime did not aim for absolute thought control as operated by a totalitarian state. Instead, it sought to depoliticize society. By combining co-optation with depoliticization, the administration for five years (2014–2019) effectively controlled civil society, suppressed street politics, and avoided confrontation with the masses that could potentially lead to a popular uprising. As the literature on the post–Cold War military politics points out, military regimes that base their power upon co-optation and institutional mechanisms, not merely violent suppression, tend to last significantly longer than those using personalized rule and intensive coercive tactics (see Boix and Svolik 2013; Gandhi and Przeworski 2006). The Prayut military regime (2014–2019) fits this pattern.

Consolidation of Royal Power

After the 2014 coup, the military thus emerged as the most powerful political entity in Thailand. Unexpectedly, before long, the monarchy also began to reassert itself. The Thai political order shifted in October 2016 with the passing of King Bhumibol Adulyadej, the longest-reigning monarch in the history of Thailand. He reigned for seventy years, was served by a total of thirty prime ministers, and was popular, even revered. Under his kingship, the palace had built a network of influence linked through various military, bureaucratic, and business elites. Over time, this "network monarchy" had become the most powerful political network in the country, effectively shaping the Thai political order (Charnvit 2020; McCargo 2005; McCargo 2021). Since ascending to the throne in 2016, amidst the political crisis caused by the 2014 coup, King Vajiralongkorn, the only son of King Bhumibol, has taken a new pathway of royal leadership, ruling the country and the palace in a different manner. He has taken several actions to expand his personal power over political, military, and economic affairs (Chambers 2019; Supalak 2022).

For example, one unexpected change regarding royal assets took place in July 2017 when an amendment regarding the CPB Act was passed. With this amendment, King Vajiralongkorn reorganized the CPB to provide him with absolute and personal control over the assets of the monarchy. With this historic change, the first structural change in the CPB since the 1940s, the king directly appoints and removes board members of the Bureau. During King Bhumibol's reign, even though the activities of the CPB had not been scrutinized by the public, its board of directors was officially under the supervision of the Finance Ministry. The new law legally and practically makes the CPB independent of the government and under the personal control of the monarch. By 2011, the estimated wealth of the CPB was US$30 billion, and King Vajiralongkorn's shares in the Siam Commercial Bank and Siam Cement Group, two prominent Thai corporations, were valued at about US$9–10 billion in total. According to research on the wealth of Thai elites, "clearly, the royal family would be ranked at the pinnacle of Thailand's richest lists" (Hewison 2019, 3; see also Puangchon 2019).

The new king also began to take a keen interest in police and military affairs. Experts have observed "a palace intent on personalizing its own control over the army as well as the police" (Chambers 2020). Gradually, there has been a move toward the appointment of senior police favorable to the palace since the new reign began in 2016. In October 2018, crucially, a new special police division was established, the Ratchawallop Police Retainers, also known as Kings Guard 904, to protect the monarchy. This special unit is not under the control of the Royal Thai Police. Instead, it is directly controlled by the King and enjoys enormous power in suppressing dissidents suspected of being disloyal to the monarchy (Chambers 2020).

The most significant development was the direct assertion of palace control over the military. In October 2019, King Vajiralongkorn ordered the transfer of two army units, the Bangkok-based 1st and 11th Infantry Regiments, from the military chain of command to the direct command of the palace. This transfer of authority covered personnel management, responsibility for training and security, and operational budgets. According to the constitution, the king is technically the commander-in-chief of all of Thailand's armed units, but the new decree bypasses the usual military chain of command. These two army units are key strategic units of the First Army region, which includes Bangkok and central Thailand, and historically have been positioned as the two most important forces responsible for ensuring the success of coup attempts. The two powerful units will now directly report to the king, who heads the Royal Security Command. Similar to police affairs, there has also been a move toward the appointment of senior military figures close to the palace in annual military reshuffles since 2016 (Supalak 2022).

The late King Bhumibol exercised power discreetly behind the scenes through a vast network of people surrounding the palace and was rarely directly and/or openly involved in politics. Today, by wielding monarchical power openly and directly over political, military, and economic activities, the palace has made itself more vulnerable to public criticism, which in turn could weaken the popularity and legitimacy of the regal institution.

More importantly, the consolidation of personal authority of the monarch might not bode well for democratic development. The palace, supported and protected by the army and the lèse majesté law, wields enormous influence over public affairs but is situated above public criticism (Haberkorn 2021; Streckfuss 2020). This situation undermines modern principles such as the separation of powers, people's sovereignty, rule of law, and public accountability. In the past, strong ties between the palace and the military have effectively established the most powerful alliance in the political system and conditioned the success of military coups that have overthrown democratically elected governments. Political interventions by the royal-military alliance have been by far the most decisive factor causing democratic breakdown in Thailand. The strong assertion of royal power under the new reign puts Thailand at a greater risk of unlawful intervention by the royal-military forces.

However, post-2014, there was also a growing pushback against autocratization under the military-monarchy alliance by pro-democratic forces. In the 2019 election, the first election since the 2014 coup and the first election under the new reign, Thai society witnessed a novel political dynamic with the emergence of new political players and social cleavages. There were concerted efforts within the opposition to unseat Prayut and push for a transition to democracy using the electoral process. However, direct interference by the monarchy, military, and judiciary shaped the electoral outcome and prolonged the autocratic rule of Prayut and his coup coalition.

The Unfree and Unfair 2019 Elections: Contestation under Military Rule and an Undemocratic Constitution

On March 24, 2019, Thailand held its first national elections in eight years. These polls came half a decade after the 2014 military coup that ushered in the longest period of military rule since the 1970s. The elections took place against the backdrop of a country that remained deeply polarized politically and highly unequal socioeconomically. The stakes were high, as the election would determine not merely who would lead the next government, but the very form of Thailand's political system. The palace and military elites were clearly looking to consolidate their hold on power by establishing a stable semi-authoritarian regime. Within such a regime, the formal electoral process would be used to defuse domestic political pressures and to earn greater international legitimacy than had been possible under direct military rule. Of the roughly 51 million people eligible to vote in 2019, 7 million were young voters eligible for the first time. Eighty parties and 13,310 candidates contested, a record in Thai polling history (Hataikarn 2019). They covered a broad ideological spectrum, from progressive parties advocating the creation of a welfare state and radical decentralization to pro-military and royalist parties.

Electoral Manipulation and Intimidation

In the lead-up to the elections, the NCPO, led by Prayut, attempted several measures to maintain power. These included introducing a new electoral system that would reduce the seats controlled by Thaksin-aligned parties, appointing a new set of election commissioners, and distributing state resources to millions of poor voters through various government schemes. Fundamentally, however, the NCPO chose the same strategy of winning power through elections as had past juntas: It relied on provincial bosses with local influence (*jao pho*), as well as established politicians (in this case, including many formerly aligned with Thaksin Shinawatra's network) to establish an ad-hoc party, Palang Pracharat. Furthermore, the junta interfered in the electoral process in ways designed to maintain its rule, including through gerrymandering designed to benefit Palang Pracharat and manipulating the design of the ballot paper (*The Nation*, November 23, 2018).

The new electoral rules the junta introduced were complicated, and most voters did not fully understand the voting system. This new system, as previously explained, was designed to prevent the Pheu Thai Party associated with Thaksin from winning a landslide victory. Voters would elect 500 lower house members, while the junta would appoint 250 senators. In a joint session, the prime minister, not required to be a member of parliament, would be selected, aiming to facilitate Prayut's return to power.

Electoral intimidation, meanwhile, was pervasive. There were severe restrictions on campaigning and heavy interference by the NCPO in the conduct of the elections. The NCPO's near absolute power created a climate of fear where freedom of expression and assembly was curtailed. Overall, the campaign environment was heavily tilted to benefit the junta and the candidates that it supported (Ricks 2019; Siripan 2020). There was evidence of pro-democracy rallies being banned, activists being arrested, and campaign rallies of non-regime parties being obstructed. In fiercely contested constituencies, there were several reports of security officers directing harassment and intimidation toward anti-junta politicians and supporters. Candidates from Pheu Thai, Future Forward, and the Democrat parties reported that police and military personnel searched their houses without warrants. Both international and domestic observers had limitations imposed on their access to polling stations and tabulation centers. Local officials in certain areas harassed domestic poll observers (*Matichon*, March 24, 2019; ANFREL 2019).

In addition to the uneven playing field, there were significant irregularities in the electoral process. According to one election monitoring group, the "tabulation and consolidation of ballots were deeply flawed, which led to an announcement of some preliminary results that were wildly inaccurate" (ANFREL 2019). Discrepancies in poll figures appeared in many constituencies. Despite strong demands by political parties and civil-society groups, the Election Commission refused to release comprehensive election data from each polling station. Voters thus felt collective frustration regarding the perceived incompetence and lack of transparency of the election commission. (An online campaign demanding the impeachment of the election commission gathered almost one million signatures in two days, making it the largest online campaign in Thai history.) By all accounts, suffice it to say that the 2019 election was Thailand's least free and fair election since the political reform of 1997.

Elite Intervention: A New Reign, Shifting Networks, and Ideological Contestation

As well as being generally unfree, the 2019 election was also not a normal election involving only the competing political parties. Other actors on the Thai political scene shaped the electoral outcome. These actors included, most notably, the monarchy and the army. The February 8 "political earthquake," which saw the announcement that the king's sister, Princess Ubolratana, would be a prime ministerial candidate and the rapid retraction of this announcement after the king intervened, reflected that the so-called "network monarchy" was undergoing a significant transformation, becoming both more fractured and more willing to intervene openly in the political process (Johnson 2019). On February 8, Thai Raksa Chart, a Thaksin-aligned party, stated it would nominate former Princess Ubolratana Mahidol, as a prime ministerial candidate. That night, the King made an announcement, which was televised nationwide, indicating that his sister's candidacy was "highly inappropriate" and would "violate the royal tradition" because royal family members were supposed to be "above politics" (*Matichon*, February 8, 2019). The royal announcement was followed by an Election Commission decision to deny Ubolratana permission to run, and a Constitutional Court ruling to dissolve the Thai Raksa Chart over its naming her for the premiership. Even so, the shocking political deal made between Ubolratana and Thaksin revealed that Thaksin retained considerable clout and pointed toward breaks within network monarchy. Direct involvement of royal family members in an electoral contest was unprecedented in Thailand. This event thus stirred public discussion on the role of the monarchy in Thai politics and on the inner workings of the royal family (Prajak 2019d).

The military was also strongly involved during the election campaign. General Apirat Kongsompong, an arch-royalist army chief, took several actions against anti-junta parties. He also ordered 800 senior military officials to attend a public oath-swearing ceremony where they vowed to only serve a government that was loyal to the monarchy. After the election, he made other provocative comments against the Future Forward Party (FFP), which, as we shall see, campaigned strongly on an anti-military and anti-establishment platform (*The Nation*, April 3, 2019).

Two days prior to the election, Thaksin orchestrated another symbolic political move by publicizing photos showing intimate "hugging" between him and Ubolratana at his daughter's wedding in Hong Kong. The so-called "Hong Kong effect" angered the establishment and conservative Thais who viewed this relationship between the exiled former prime minister and princess as an unacceptable provocation. A day later, and just hours before the polls opened, the king issued a rare and surprising statement urging Thai voters to elect "good people" to govern the country. Subsequently, the election commission president and army chief asked voters to consider the king's advice, saying that following this advice would keep the country peaceful and stable (*The Nation*, March 24, 2019). In Thailand, "good people" is a political code phrase commonly used to refer to anti-Thaksin political groups and politicians who adhere to official ideology emphasizing the "nation, religion, and king." Rather than settling political conflict, the involvement of the monarchy, the military, judiciary, and Thaksin and his supporters turned this election into another arena for ideological contestation.

Polarized Voting and the Youth Awakening

The parties contesting in the 2019 elections can roughly be divided into three political categories: pro-regime, led by the Palang Pracharat Party (PPRP); anti-regime, led by Pheu Thai and Future Forward; and fence-sitting, led by the Democrat Party and Bhumjaithai. An emerging new player was the FFP, which was led by the young charismatic businessman Thanathorn Juangroongruangkit, who was immensely popular among young voters. The results showed that no political camp had a clear majority. Old parties like Pheu Thai and the Democrat Party struggled to retain support, whereas new parties, notably PPRP and Future Forward, performed better than expected. There were contradictory patterns in voting behavior and electioneering. Old methods like using vote buying and vote brokers persisted, but new campaign techniques using online methods and social media were also influential. The regional pattern of voting witnessed in previous elections also changed. The Democrats lost many seats in the south and were completely eradicated in Bangkok. Pheu Thai lost their absolute control in the north and northeast. Overall, the 2019 elections demonstrated a more fragmented political landscape in Thailand.

The election result ended the pattern of two-party competition between Thaksin-aligned parties and the Democrats as witnessed from 2001 to 2011. During that period, these two major parties combined gained over 80 percent of parliamentary seats. This election was more competitive, with five parties (Pheu Thai, PPRP, FFP, the Democrats, and Bhumjaitai) gaining a significant number of MPs, with no strong winner. The seats of these five parties accounted for 86.8 percent of the House. With 136 seats, compared to 265 seats in 2011, Pheu Thai remained the largest party but lost its hegemonic position. Overall, support for the party decreased in almost every constituency nationwide, but it managed to keep its strongest base of support in the north and northeast (Selway and Hicken 2019).

A resounding loser in this election, by all measures, was the Democrat Party. The party's vote share and seat share plummeted significantly in every region, including in their strongholds in the south and Bangkok. The party dropped from being the second-largest party to the fourth for the first time in two decades. Its equivocal stance of not stating clearly whether it was pro- or anti-junta cost the party dearly, as did the weak leadership provided by Abhisit and party internal conflicts. The party lost votes on both flanks, losing conservative supporters to the PPRP, and losing moderate and progressive supporters to Future Forward.

The junta-backed Palang Pracharat party and the vibrant Future Forward emerged as the "winners" of this election. This outcome reflected deepening polarization. The campaigns of these two newly created parties promoted radically contrasting pro- and anti-regime platforms, respectively. After five years of military authoritarianism, Prayut had become a divisive figure, and his administration was associated with an increasing rate of poverty, widening income inequality, corruption scandals, and human rights violations. While the PPRP gained support from conservatives and older voters who favored the stability and status quo the regime provided, FFP attracted votes from a mixed group of young, urban, and entrepreneurial voters who wanted to see structural change and reform (McCargo and Anyarat 2020).

The PPRP relied largely on the co-optation of provincial bosses to build its voter base, showing that this party was sticking with old tactics. These included co-optation of former MPs from other political parties (PPRP succeeded in pulling sixty-two former MPs, nineteen former ministers, and one former senator from other parties); mobilization of vote canvassers controlled by political bosses at the local level; exploitation of systems of patronage and pork-barrel politics; and the distribution of goods and money to voters (Prajak 2019b; Siripan 2020). Even though the party fell short of achieving its anticipated 150 seats, it emerged as the largest vote-getter and second largest seat-getter (115 seats). This performance showed that local patronage networks and government intervention continue to play important roles in Thai elections, especially in rural areas. Nevertheless, PPRP was composed of several political factions with no shared vision or policy platform. The sole tie binding them together was support for Prayut's return to power. Historically in Thailand, junta-backed parties tend to be short-lived, typically experiencing internal conflict over coveted cabinet positions and government budget allocations (Prajak 2018).

The FFP leaders promised voters they would push for military reform, the elimination of big business monopolies, radical decentralization, and political restructuring through constitutional amendments. With eighty seats and the highest number of votes in Bangkok, FFP became the third largest party in Thailand and a force to be reckoned with. The party performed well not only in Bangkok, but also in central Thailand and the east – the three most affluent and urbanized regions. The party performed relatively poorly in rural constituencies in all regions. There were two main reasons why the party was not successful in the countryside: The FFP refused to use the old system of vote canvasing and its campaign relied heavily on social media, which was not a main channel for information-sharing among the rural population. The FFP leaders admitted that they were largely unable to penetrate into poor and remote areas in this election.[23] Nevertheless, the FFP campaign strategy of online outreach and social media paid off overall.

In fact, voting patterns and political debate during the campaign demonstrated that a new social cleavage was emerging in this election: a generational divide separating young and elderly voters. As previously discussed, in the past, the urban–rural divide had been a primary cleavage shaping Thai voting patterns. During 2001–2014, Thaksin's parties repeatedly gained overwhelming support in the more rural north and northeast, while the Democrats dominated in the south and among urban districts of Bangkok. This time, by several times

[23] Interview, Future Forward Party's members, May 10, 2019. The party allocated most of their time and resources to campaign in Bangkok and urban districts.

postponing the elections, the NCPO had ironically increased the number of first-time voters, to the point that youth have become a significant voting bloc accounting for 14 percent of eligible voters. And Thai millennials found their voice and representation in the FFP and its leader, Thanathorn. When the king issued a royal statement on the eve of the election urging Thais to "vote for good people," millennials swiftly responded with a Twitter hashtag that became the top-ranked trend overnight, saying, "We are grown-up now and can choose for ourselves" (McCargo 2019). The Future Forward Party gained overwhelming support from young, first-time voters, who were active users of social media (Anna 2019). The age cleavage is now set to be a crucial factor in the next election, with the FFP and Thanathorn having the demographic advantage.

The new electoral map revealed in 2019 showed that the establishment and military are now fighting on two fronts simultaneously. In rural areas, the royal-military elites have to compete with Thaksin-allied parties, which remain very strong in these areas. And they now face a new political threat posed by the FFP's Thanathorn, who is immensely popular in urban areas and among the young. In the 2019 elections, the number of votes gained by the two anti-regime parties, Pheu Thai and FFP, combined was roughly 14 million, while the pro-regime PPRP party earned only 8.4 million votes (Prajak 2019d). Clearly, the majority of voters expressed support for change.

Power Contestation: Democratic Rejuvenation and State Repression

Thai politics after the 2019 election remained highly uncertain and unstable. The election did not bring about the return to a stable, democratic system, nor did establishment and military leaders succeed in their attempt to establish a robust electoral authoritarian regime. As a result, the elections were only the beginning of a new round of struggles aimed at defining the terms of the new political order under the new reign.

After the election, with strong support from a junta-appointed Senate, the PPRP, despite not being the winning party, managed to form a coalition government of twenty small- and medium-sized parties to return Prayut to power. Ironically, Prayut's administration was a by-product of the 2017 constitution that was designed to produce a weak coalition government. The coalition government struggled to formulate and implement policies that respond to the needs of the people and the volatile world disrupted by the coronavirus outbreak. The economic hardship and the looming crisis caused by the pandemic posed tough challenges for his government. High unemployment and business bankruptcies led to public discontent. Disunity within the coalition, a result of fierce conflict among coalition parties and within the PPRP over cabinet seats, weakened the administration's capacity to resolve the crisis. As a result, the legitimacy and popularity of the government plummeted (Tita 2022).

In February 2020, the Constitutional Court dissolved the FFP and banned its executives from politics for ten years, sparking nationwide student protests.[24] Supporters of FFP, including students, perceived this court ruling as a deliberate attempt to eliminate this new opposition force and to strengthen the unpopular regime. Students mobilized for what quickly became the largest youth protest movement since the 1970s, gathering significant public support. In addition to opposing the dissolution of the FFP, the protestors also responded to socio-political factors such as escalating inequality, a repressive government, and the imposition of hyper-conservative education by the Prayut administration. Youth activists employed novel mobilization strategies, leveraging the internet and social media to disseminate information and ideas, utilizing flash mob tactics to evade police crackdowns, and innovatively engaging in symbolic politics as a tool against the autocratic regime. The youth movement in 2020 was a new form of social movement for Thailand, establishing a horizontal, pluralistic, and loosely organized structure to underscore its democratic culture (Kanokrat 2021b; Saowanee 2021). Their political demands included dissolving the parliament, respecting civil liberties, and rewriting the constitution. More importantly, the student protests went beyond Prayut and the military to criticize the monarchy directly, another new development in modern Thai politics.

Their criticism of the monarchy covered a range of critical issues, from the monarchy's role in supporting the coup and subsequent military regime, its role in violations of human rights, royal interference in police and military affairs, the enormous wealth of the king and the privatization of the Crown Property Bureau, to the king's personal behavior. In raising such issues, the youth protestors broke a sacred taboo of Thai politics, which hitherto had prevented any open discussion of the role of the monarchy in public space. Previous progressive political groups and movements used gossip, coded language, symbols, and underground communication to express criticism of the monarchy (Anonymous 2018; Ünaldi 2014). In the 2020–2021 protests, the young activists made their criticisms openly, endeavoring to shift public discourse and carve out new space for democratic deliberation. Their ultimate goal was the reform not just of the electoral political system, but also of the monarchy. According to the young protesters, the royal-military alliance and their political intervention was the root cause of Thailand's democratic regression.

---

[24] The Court reasoned that a loan that party leader Thanathorn had provided to his party could be viewed as a "concealed donation" under Section 66 of the Political Parties Act, which limits donations to 10 million baht per donor per year (*Bangkok Post*, February 21, 2020).

The royal-military elite pushed back against the call for reform by violently suppressing the protesters, intimidating activists and their families, and arresting and imprisoning protest leaders. The Prayut government extensively employed the lèse majesté law, the Computer Crime Act, and the Sedition Act to suppress youth critique of the monarchy. The most alarming instance involved a fourteen-year-old high school student who was charged with defaming the monarchy for two posts she made on Facebook.[25] These harsh tactics eventually debilitated the progressive movement of the youth.

With the support of the monarchy and military, the Prayut administration effectively quelled the protest movement, allowing Prayut to sustain his frail and unpopular coalition throughout the entirety of his four-year term. However, a formidable challenge emerged in 2023 when Prayut faced a new election amidst a landscape marked by a more robust opposition force and burgeoning anti-establishment sentiment.

A New Political Crossroads: Political Realignment after the 2023 Elections

Upon initial observation, the 2023 election mirrored that of 2019, involving a contest between pro-regime and anti-regime alliances. It was now evident that dominant monarchical-military elites were actively seeking to maintain power by engaging in electoral manipulation. Conversely, the opposition parties aimed to put an end to the undemocratic rule of Prayut. Nevertheless, the altered dynamics within the opposition force rendered this election markedly distinct from its predecessor.

The two leading opposition parties held distinct political stances and perspectives regarding democratic change. The Move Forward Party (MFP), successor to the dissolved FFP and spearheaded by the charismatic businessman Pita Limjaroenrat, strongly advocated reform in both the monarchy and the military. Party leaders emphatically stated a commitment to not forming a coalition with pro-military parties backing Prayut and Prawit. On the other hand, Pheu Thai, with Thaksin's daughter and real estate businessman Srettha Thavisin as its prime ministerial candidates, centered its campaign predominantly on economic issues, avoiding delving into discussions about fundamental political restructuring, notably steering away from the subject of monarchy reform. Pheu Thai leaders also demonstrated an ambiguous stance on whether they would join hands with parties led by former coup leaders (*Bangkok Post*, April 22, 2023). The cooperation observed between Pheu Thai and the MFP in 2019 was

[25] See Jintamas Saksornchai, "Thai police arrest 2nd teenager for defaming monarchy amid renewed debate over rigorous law," *AP News*, May 17, 2023.

supplanted this time around by intense competition between these two parties, both of which were vying for votes from a shared pool of voters discontented with the government.

Two pro-military parties competed in the 2023 general elections: the PPRP, led by General Prawit Wongsuwan, and the newly created United Thai Nation Party (UTN), led by outgoing Prime Minister General Prayut Chan-ocha. Ahead of the 2023 polls, Prawit and Prayut's personal ambitions to lead the government created a rift between these two generals and conflict among their supporters. After assisting Prayut for nine years, Prawit, who is more senior, aspired to take the helm himself. Prayut and his backers, therefore, split from the PPRP and formed the UTN, using Prayut's royalist image to court conservative voters. However, due to Prayut's waning popularity stemming from his prolonged tenure as prime minister and his government's lackluster handling of the economy, the UTN struggled to attract first-rate politicians. Meanwhile, Prawit's faction maintained control over the PPRP, relying extensively on the same strategies it had employed in 2019 (Prajak 2023).

The results indicated a clear rejection of Prayut and junta leaders by a majority of voters. Pro-military parties performed poorly, while the opposition garnered substantial support. The PPRP came in fourth, with only forty seats, while the UTN won just thirty-six seats. The progressive anti-regime MFP achieved an unexpected victory, surpassing expectations that Pheu Thai would win. The MFP secured 151 MP seats and 14.23 million party-list votes. They dominated in Bangkok, losing only one seat to Pheu Thai, and received impressive party-list votes in the traditionally conservative southern regions. Pheu Thai, on the other hand, claimed the second position with 141 seats and only 10.96 million party-list votes, the lowest in the history of Thaksin party vehicles. It experienced significant losses in party strongholds in the north and northeast. In Chiang Mai, Thaksin's birthplace, Pheu Thai conceded several constituencies to the MFP. It is noteworthy that this election was the first defeat of Pheu Thai since its establishment in 2001 (Hicken and Napon 2023).

The remarkable success of the MFP signifies the resilience of pro-democratic forces in Thailand. Between 2019 and 2023, the progressive, pro-reform movement actively pushed back against the trend toward autocratization, employing both street mobilizations and electoral processes. After enduring years of democratic backsliding and ineffective governance, members of the Thai population desiring substantial change found that they had a representative in the progressive MFP. This shift positioned the MFP as a new threat to the political establishment. Meanwhile, the defeat of the PPRP and UTN underscores that while local networks of influence and patronage still hold some sway in elections, they alone are insufficient to secure electoral victory. Moreover, while embracing an ultra-royalist and militarist ideology might attract a limited segment of conservative voters, the majority of the electorate rejects that strategy.

The electoral setbacks these two parties experienced underscore the challenges Thailand's royalist and conservative elites face in sustaining their political dominance through electoral processes. Historically, the deficiencies exhibited by both parties are not anomalous; rather, they align with the persistent vulnerabilities observed in pro-junta governments in Thailand. The nation's authoritarian leaders have consistently encountered difficulties in establishing strong and durable party-based regimes.

The defeat of both the PPRP and UTN diminished the prospects of junta leaders retaining power. Nevertheless, undemocratic elements within the junta-crafted 2017 constitution allowed parties aligned with the military to participate in the new coalition government. Initially, the MFP, securing the highest number of seats, spearheaded a coalition comprising eight parties. However, Pita Limjaroenrat, the leader of the MFP, faced failure in his attempt to assume the role of prime minister, as junta-appointed senators opposed his appointment during a parliamentary vote. The senators expressed concerns over the perceived threat the MFP allegedly posed to Thailand's three sacred pillars of nation, religion, and monarchy. Major political parties, including PPRP and UTN, publicly criticized the MFP on similar grounds, announcing their refusal to join any coalition that included the MFP (Ratcliffe and Navaon 2023). Consequently, the party found itself marginalized within mainstream politics.

These methods allowed royal-military elites to successfully block the MFP from assuming power. Instead, a controversial coalition between pro-military parties and Pheu Thai formed with the backing of conservative elites. This unlikely alliance demonstrated the ability of royal-military elites to sustain their power despite electoral setbacks, benefiting, of course, from the political structures established following the 2014 military coup. The military-appointed Senate, Election Commission, and Constitutional Court acted as gatekeepers for the traditional elites. In turn, these elites co-opted Pheu Thai by offering Thaksin, in exile since 2008, a safe return to the country with a royal pardon, as well as by endorsing Pheu Thai's Srettha Thavisin for the position of prime minister.

The new coalition government led by Pheu Thai affirmed that it would not pursue amendments to the lèse majesté law or constitutional changes that would alter monarchical powers (*Bangkok Post*, July 20, 2023). It has exercised great political caution, avoiding saying anything that might disturb royal-military elites. As a result, the aftermath of the 2023 elections highlights how these royal-military elites are able to obstruct democratic transition and maintain power by relying on undemocratic institutions, without the need for electoral victory.

6 Conclusion

This Element has presented an overview of change and continuity in Thai politics, spanning the era of military authoritarian rule in the late 1950s to the present period of political division that began with the ascent of Thaksin. The depiction of modern Thai politics these pages present is of a highly contested polity – one characterized by persistent conflict, recurrent instability, and frequent regime changes. Not all political leaders and social groups embrace democracy as the established premise of the political game. Instead, Thai society has witnessed numerous instances of democratic breakdown and backsliding, including in the present moment, triggered by military coups, executive aggrandizement, tumultuous street politics, and judicial activism.

Nevertheless, elites have never fully achieved their goal of establishing an enduring autocratic form of rule. Civil society has demonstrated resilience, giving rise to movements that repeatedly challenge undemocratic rules and authoritarian conduct. On many occasions, popular uprisings have overthrown military regimes; protestors have eroded the legitimacy of illiberal leaders, and popular parties have defeated military-backed parties, paving the way for episodes of liberalization and democratic transition. To comprehend Thai politics is to grasp the fundamentally contested nature of this polity.

This instability, and the frequent changes in regime, can be attributed to the absence of any political actors able to successfully establish absolute control over the polity. Consequently, we observe a continual struggle for power among diverse groups, movements, and networks. The political actions of both elites and mass movements have been shaped by socioeconomic changes, institutional rules, and ideological shifts. Throughout each period, this Element has elucidated key conflicts within the elite class and the challenges they confront as a result of the emergence of new social groups and political movements. Additionally, it has scrutinized how the elites have addressed these challenges through mechanisms such as repression, institutional manipulation, mobilization of mass support, and co-optation of opponents into their own networks of power.

Prior to the 1973 democratic uprising, the military elite wielded dominance, routinely using coups to eliminate rivals and seize state power. Once in control, elections were conducted as political rituals to legitimize military rule. The military employed various tools, both legal and illegal, to limit genuine competition and secure victory, including under the rubric of culturally appropriate

"Thai-style democracy." A pivotal development occurred under General Sarit Thanarat when the military decided to revive the monarchy to garner support for military rule. Recognizing the symbolic power and political capital of the monarchy, Sarit's political strategy marked a crucial turning point in Thai politics. Subsequently, the monarchy-military partnership emerged as the most potent political alliance in the kingdom. Over time, King Bhumibol Adulyadej, with the backing of his royalist network and allied military leaders, accumulated political capital, expanded his sphere of power, and became involved in political affairs.

A political shift occurred with the fall of the military regime resulting from a mass uprising led by students in 1973, marking the establishment of parliamentary democracy as a replacement for authoritarian bureaucratic politics. In this new but constantly evolving political landscape, electoral politics gained significance as a primary avenue for attaining power and wealth. This shift presented opportunities and incentives for business leaders to enter politics, both in Bangkok and provincial areas. Founding political parties, they secured substantial access to state power. However, key ministries related to national security and the premiership remained under the control of the military and royalist elites. Despite challenges and opposition following the democratic transition in 1973, the royal-military alliance adapted and sustained its dominance by combining repression with the influence of a semi-democratic constitution and co-optation of the new breed of businesspeople-turned-politicians.

Another crucial turning point came in 1997 when the financial crisis that year triggered a decade of transformation and turbulence. During this time, parliamentary democracy and electoral institutions underwent significant changes. Initially, the 1997 constitution and political reforms resulted in a robust and stable civilian administration and political party structure, with Thaksin Shinawatra dominating the national political stage. Programmatic politics and policy-based campaigning gained prominence in shaping electoral outcomes, though without completely displacing patronage and other old techniques of campaigning. Parties and electoral institutions became stronger, and ordinary citizens became more politically engaged.

The traditional royal-military alliance, extremely concerned about their declining influence but unwilling to engage in electoral competition, resorted to an antiquated military coup to oust Thaksin's democratically elected government. The 2006 coup heightened polarization and intensified political conflict. From 2006 to 2014, Thai politics was characterized by competition between two prominent networks: the "network monarchy" centered around the monarch and the "Thaksin network," centered on the populist leader. Each network invoked competing sources of legitimacy: traditional authority and popular mandate. Their conflict drew on deep-seated social cleavages, particularly those based on urban–rural disparities and income inequality, but was exacerbated by an intense elite power struggle. Both pro- and anti-Thaksin camps resorted to mass mobilization, using confrontational and disruptive tactics, leading to violent color-coded politics. Thailand experienced deep democratic recession. However, despite the royal-military elites' use of a range of repressive strategies to preserve their grip on power and subdue Thaksin's political machine and the Red Shirt movement, they were not entirely successful in eliminating these formidable forces that challenged their authority.

In 2014, the royal-military alliance initiated another coup to consolidate their authority. This coup, orchestrated by General Prayut, and the transition to a new king in 2016 following the passing of King Bhumibol, marked the beginning of a new era. Under the new monarch, the network monarchy entered a phase of critical transition. Since ascending to the throne in 2016, King Vajiralongkorn has adopted a distinctive style of royal leadership, governing the country in a novel manner. He has implemented several measures to enhance his personal influence over political, military, and economic affairs. Meanwhile, the trajectory of Thai democratic backsliding extended throughout Prayut's prolonged tenure, supported by both the military and the palace. The ruling junta, led by General Prayut and General Pravit Wongsuwan, sought to fortify the influence of royal-military power by recentralizing power and designing a new political framework, distilled in the 2017 constitution, that was strategically designed to curb majoritarian democracy and diminish the influence of political parties.

These measures did not stabilize Thai politics. Pro-democratic forces effectively countered both through a new wave of protests in 2020–2021, during which young activists mobilized (unsuccessfully) to topple Prayut and advocate for monarchy reform, and through two elections. In 2019, young voters and the opposition coalition, led by Pheu Thai and the FFP, attempted to oust Prayut through the ballot box. However, intervention by the monarchy, military, and judiciary defused the electoral outcome and extended Prayut's autocratic rule. In 2023, a new election unequivocally signaled widespread rejection of Prayut and junta leaders by the majority of voters. Pro-military parties experienced a notable decline in performance, while opposition parties, particularly the MFP and Pheu Thai, secured the majority of votes. The MFP, a young and progressive party, achieved particular success. However, royal-military elites again used undemocratic mechanisms embedded in the 2017 constitution to prevent the election from delivering change and prevented the MFP from assuming power. Instead, an unconventional coalition emerged between pro-military parties and Pheu Thai, highlighting the royal-military elites' ability to maintain power despite electoral setbacks.

What insights can we glean from this examination of political transformations in Thailand?

A considerable portion of recent literature on regime change and democratic backsliding posits that in the contemporary world, the principal catalyst for the demise of democracy is not traditional military coups but, rather, what is termed "executive aggrandizement." Democracies face peril when popularly elected leaders undermine media freedoms and judicial autonomy, erode civil liberties, and weaken mechanisms of democratic accountability as well as checks and balances, while maintaining a popular mandate (Bermeo 2016; Levitsky and Ziblatt 2018). However, Thai political experience diverges from this trend. While executive aggrandizement manifested to a certain extent under the Thaksin administration (2001–2006), the enduring and more serious threat to Thai democracy remains the old-fashioned military coup, and an elite that is determined to remain in power despite, not as a result of, electoral outcomes.

As long as the traditional elites remain committed to preserving "Thai-style democracy," characterized by despotic paternalism and royal-military authoritarianism, the potential for political instability will persist. The royal-military alliance does not embrace the fundamental democratic principle of political equality, viewing it as contradicting the traditional hierarchical structure of Thai society. These conservative elites retain control over crucial elements of the state apparatus, including the military, the judiciary, and certain segments of the bureaucracy, and are willing to use them to secure their dominance. Consequently, they possess the capability to impede democratic progress when they perceive their status and power as under threat, as evidenced by the coups in 2006 and 2014.

However, the royal-military alliance has adapted to prevailing global democratic norms, recognizing that seizing state power through military coups is not a sustainable approach. Acknowledging the need for at least a democratic façade to secure legitimacy, they have actively participated in drafting constitutions and manipulating the electoral process to embed their power in the system. Beyond relying on coercive force to suppress opposition, they have repeatedly employed legal mechanisms, including Constitutional Court rulings, to intimidate and weaken pro-democratic forces. They have also used the politics of cooptation, offering rewards and positions to adversaries to neutralize them; the temporary alliances forged between royalist elites and Thaksin thus represent a recurring pattern. Ultimately, addressing and resolving the issue of royal-military interference in politics will be crucial for building a stable and well-functioning democracy in Thailand.

While the dominant royal-military alliance has shown both adaptability and tenacity, it should also be stressed that Thai democracy has experienced rejuvenation over time, demonstrating capacity for resilience. It has never faced permanent demise. Socioeconomic changes have repeatedly given rise to new social groups and ideologies that have mounted recurrent challenges to the political establishment. The 1970s witnessed the rise of students, labor unions, and farmers' movements, followed by the increasing role of business and the middle class in the 1980s and 1990s. New grassroots movements mobilized after the 1997 political reforms, including among the rural poor, while recent resistance to military-dominated government has seen an awakening among youth and a new democratic movement. The political aspirations and resilience of the contemporary young generation are deeply rooted in long-standing traditions of civil-society activism and participatory politics in Thailand.

While it is impossible to predict how or when the contemporary political stalemate will end, we can conclude from the foregoing analysis that the Thai polity continues to be a site of fierce contestation. Thai politics is never static and evokes both despair and hope.

References

Newspapers and Magazines

Bangkok Post
Isara News
Khao Sod
Manager Daily
Matichon
Post Today
Prachachat Thurakij
Thai PBS News
The Nation

Books, Monographs, and Articles

Acemoglu, Daron and James Robinson. 2006. *Economic Origins of Dictatorship and Democracy*. Cambridge: Cambridge University Press.

Aim Sinpeng. 2021. *Opposing Democracy in the Digital Age: The Yellow Shirts in Thailand*. Michigan: University of Michigan Press.

Anderson, Benedict. 1977. "Withdrawal Symptoms: Social and Cultural Aspects of the October 6 Coup." *Bulletin of Concerned Asian Scholars*, 9(3): 13–30.

Anderson, Benedict. 1990. "Murder and Progress in Modern Siam." *New Left Review*, 181 (May–June): 33–48.

Anek Laothamatas. 1992. *Business Associations and the New Political Economy of Thailand: From Bureaucratic Polity to Liberal Corporatism*. Boulder, CO: Westview Press, Institute of Southeast Asian Studies.

ANFREL. 2019. Asian Network for Free Election's interim report. https://anfrel.org/wp-content/uploads/2019/03/ANFREL-Thailand-Interim-Report-English-2.0–1.pdf (accessed October 12, 2021).

Anna Lawattanatrakul. 2019. "A country for the young: first-time voters in the 2019 general election and how they can change the face of Thai politics." *Prachatai English*, March 23. https://prachatai.com/english/node/7984.

Anonymous. 2018. "Anti-Royalism in Thailand Since 2006: Ideological Shifts and Resistance." *Journal of Contemporary Asia*, 48(3): 363–394.

Apichart Sathitniramai, Yukti Mukdawijitra, Niti Pawakapan, et al. 2013. *Phum mi that lae kanmueang khong kan phatthana chonnabot thai ruam samai*

[Landscape and Politics of Contemporary Rural Development]. Chiang Mai: Public Policy Studies Institute.

Arghiros, Daniel. 2001. *Democracy, Development and Decentralization in Provincial Thailand*. London; New York: RoutledgeCurzon.

Asa Kumpha. 2021. **กว่า จะ ครอง อำนาจ นำ** [To achieve royal hegemony]. Nonthaburi: Same Sky Book.

Bello, Walden, Shea Cunningham and Kheng Poh Li. 1999. *A Siamese Tragedy: Development and Disintegration in Modern Thailand*. Oakland: Food First Books.

Bermeo, Nancy. 2016. "On Democratic Backsliding." *Journal of Democracy*, 27(1): 5–19.

Boix, Carles and Milan Svolik. 2013. "The Foundations of Limited Authoritarian Government: Institutions and Power-Sharing in Dictatorships." *The Journal of Politics*, 75(2): 300–316.

Bowie, Katherine. 1997. *Rituals of National Identity: An Anthropology of the State and the Village Scout Movement in Thailand*. New York: Columbia University Press.

Brown, Andrew. 2004. *Labour Politics and the State in Industrializing Thailand*. New York: RoutledgeCurzon.

Brownlee, Jason. 2007. *Authoritarianism in an Age of Democratization*. Cambridge: Cambridge University Press.

Callaghy, Thomas M. 1984. *The State-Society Struggle: Zaire in Comparative Perspective*. New York: Columbia University Press.

Callahan, William. 1998. *Imaginary Democracy: Reading "The Events of May" in Thailand*. Singapore: ISEAS.

Callahan, William. 2005. "The Discourse of Vote Buying and Political Reforms in Thailand." *Pacific Affairs*, 78(1): 95–113.

Carothers, Thomas, and Andrew O'Donohue, eds. 2019. *Democracies Divided: The Global Challenge of Political Polarization*. Washington, DC: The Brookings Institution.

Case, William. 2006. "Manipulative Skills: How Do Rulers Control the Electoral Arena?" in *Electoral Authoritarianism: The Dynamics of Unfree Competition*, edited by Andreas Schedler, pp. 95–112. London: Lynne Rienner.

Case, William. 2010. *Contemporary Authoritarianism in Southeast Asia: Structures, Institutions, and Agency*. New York: Routledge.

Chai-anan Samudavanija. 1989. "Democracy in Thailand: A Case of a Stable Semi-democratic Regime." *World Affairs*, 150(1): 31–41.

Chaiwat Satha-Anand. 2006. "Fostering 'Authoritarian Democracy' with Violence: The Effect of Violent Solutions in Southern Thailand." In *Empire and Neoliberalism in Asia*, edited by Vedi R. Hadiz, pp. 169–187. London: Routledge.

Chaiyon Praditsil and Olarn Thinbangtieo. 2008. "Crisis Fallout and Political Conflict in Rayong." In *Thai Capital after the 1997 Crisis*, edited by Pasuk Phongpaichit and Chris Baker, pp. 189–214. Chiang Mai: Silkworm Books.

Chambers, Paul. 2019. "Scrutinising Thailand's 2019 annual military reshuffle." *New Mandala*, September 25, www.newmandala.org/scrutinising-thailands-2019-annual-military-reshuffle/ (accessed June 15, 2021).

Chambers, Paul. 2020. "The partisan history of police power in Thailand." *New Mandala*, March 2. www.newmandala.org/the-partisan-history-of-police-power-in-thailand/.

Chambers, Paul and Napisa Waitoolkiat. 2016. "The Resilience of Monarchised Military in Thailand." *Journal of Contemporary Asia*, 46(3): 425–444.

Charnvit Kasetsiri. 2020. "King Bhumibol Adulyadej and the Neo-monarchy of Thailand." In *Coup, King, Crisis: A Critical Interregnum in Thailand*, edited by Pavin Chachavalpongpun. New Haven, CT: Yale University Council on Southeast Asia Studies.

Connors, Michael. 2002. "Framing the 'People's Constitution'." In *Reforming Thai Politics*, edited by Duncan McCargo, pp. 37–56. Copenhagen: NIAS Press.

Derpanopoulos, George, Erica Frantz, Barbara Geddes, and Joseph Wright. 2016. "Are Coups Good for Democracy?" *Research and Politics*, 3(1) January–March: 1–7.

Donor, Richard and Ansil Ramsay. 2000. "Rent-seeking and Economic Development in Thailand." In *Rents, Rent-Seeking and Economic Development: Theory and Evidence in Asia*, edited by Mushtaq Khan and Jomo Kwame Sundaram, pp. 145–174. Cambridge: Cambridge University Press.

Donor, Richard and Ansil Ramsay. 2003. "The Challenges of Economic Upgrading in Liberalising Thailand." In *States in the Global Economy: Bringing Domestic Institutions Back In*, edited by Linda Weiss, pp.121–141. Cambridge: Cambridge University Press.

Dressel, Björn and Khemthong Tonsakulrungruang. 2019. "Coloured Judgements? The Work of the Thai Constitutional Court, 1998–2016." *Journal of Contemporary Asia*, 49(1): 1–23.

Ferrara, Federico. 2015. *The Political Development of Modern Thailand*. Cambridge: Cambridge University Press.

Gandhi, Jennifer and Adam Przeworski. 2006. "Cooperation, Cooptation and Rebellion under Dictatorships." *Economics and Politics*, 18(1): 1–26.

Geddes, Barbara, Joseph Wright, and Erica Frantz. 2018. *How Dictatorships Work*. New York: Cambridge University Press.

Glassman, Jim. 2010. "From Reds to Red Shirts: Political Evolution and Devolution in Thailand." *Environment and Planning A: Economy and Space*, 42(4): 765–770.

Haberkorn, Tyrell. 2011. *Revolution Interrupted: Farmers, Students, Law, and Violence in Northern Thailand*. Madison, WI: University of Wisconsin Press.

Haberkorn, Tyrell. 2014. "Martial Law and the Criminalization of Thought in Thailand." *The Asia-Pacific Journal: Japan Focus*, 12(40): 1–17.

Haberkorn, Tyrell. 2021. "Under and beyond the Law: Monarchy, Violence, and History in Thailand." *Politics & Society*, 49(3): 311–336.

Haggard, Stephan and Robert Kaufman. 2021. *Backsliding: Democratic Regress in the Contemporary World*. Cambridge: Cambridge University Press.

Handley, Paul. 2006. *The King Never Smiles: A Biography of Thailand's Bhumibol Adulyadej*. New Haven, CT: Yale University Press.

Hataikarn Treesuwan. 2019. "The 2019 elections: 1 month after the elections what have Thai people known." *BBC Thai*, April 24, www.bbc.com/thai/thailand-48034292 (accessed May 1, 2021).

Hewison, Kevin. 1989. *Bankers and Bureaucrats: Capital and the Role of the State in Thailand*. New Haven, CT: Yale University Council on Southeast Asian Studies.

Hewison, Kevin. 2012. "Class, Inequality, and Politics." In *Bangkok, May 2010: Perspectives on a Divided Thailand*, edited by Michael Montesano, Pavin Chachavalponqpun, and Aekapol Chongvilaivan, pp. 143–160. Singapore: Institute of Southeast Asian Studies.

Hewison, Kevin. 2019. "Crazy Rich Thais: Thailand's Capitalist Class, 1980–2019." *Journal of Contemporary Asia*, 51(1): 1–16.

Hewison, Kevin and Maniemai Thongyou. 1993. *The New Generation of Provincial Business People in Northern Thailand*. Perth: Murdoch University Asia Research Centre.

Hicken, Allen. 2006. "Party Fabrication: Constitutional Reform and the Rise of Thai Rak Thai." *Journal of East Asian Studies*, 6: 381–407.

Hicken, Allen. 2007. "How Effective Are Institutional Reforms?" In *Elections for Sale: The Causes and Consequences of Vote Buying*, edited by Frederic Charles Schaffer, pp. 145–160. Boulder, CO: Lynne Rienner.

Hicken, Allen and Napon Jatusripitak. 2023. "Introduction: Making Sense of Thailand's Seismic Elections." *Contemporary Southeast Asia*, 45(3): 335–344.

Human Right Watch. 2008. "Thailand's 'war on drugs'." International Harm Reduction Association and Human Rights Watch briefing paper, March 12 www.hrw.org/news/2008/03/12/thailands-war-drugs (accessed on February 9, 2024).

Hutchcroft, Paul. 1998. *Booty Capitalism: The Politics of Banking in the Philippines*. Ithaca, NY: Cornell University.

International Crisis Group. 2010. Bridging Thailand's deep divide, Asia report no.192, July 5. www.crisisgroup.org/asia/south-east-asia/thailand/bridging-thailand-s-deep-divide.

Janjira Sombatpoonsiri. 2020. "'Authoritarian Civil Society': How Anti-democracy Activism Shapes Thailand's Autocracy." *Journal of Civil Society*, 16(4): 333–350.

Johnson, Andrew. 2019. "New networks in Thai royal politics." *New Mandala*, February 21, 2019 www.newmandala.org/new-networks-in-thai-royal-polit ics/ (accessed April 30, 2021).

Kanda Naknoi. 2021 "The Economic Role of the Thai Military: A Commercial Logic to Coups?" In *Praetorians, Profiteers or Professionals?: Studies on the Militaries of Myanmar and Thailand*, edited by Michael J. Montesano, Terence Chong, and Prajak Kongkirati, pp. 132–149. Singapore: ISEAS–Yusof Ishak Institute.

Kanokrat Lertchoosakul. 2021a. "The Paradox of the Thai Middle Class in Democratisation." *TRaNS: Trans-Regional and -National Studies of Southeast Asia*, 9(1): 65–79.

Kanokrat Lertchoosakul. 2021b. "The White Ribbon Movement: High School Students in the 2020 Thai Youth Protests." *Critical Asian Studies*, 53(2): 206–218.

Kasian Tejapira. 2001. *Commodifying Marxism: The Formation of Modern Thai Radical Culture, 1927–1958*. Kyoto: Kyoto University Press.

Kasian Tejapira. 2006. "Toppling Thaksin." *New Left Review*, 39: 5–37.

Keyes, Charles. 2012. "'Cosmopolitan' Villagers and Populist Democracy in Thailand," *South East Asia Research*, 20(3): 343–360.

Keyes, Charles. 2014. *Finding Their Voice: Northeastern Villagers and the Thai State*. Chiang Mai: Silkworm.

Kuhonta, Eric. 2008. "The Paradox of Thailand's 1997 'People's Constitution': Be Careful What You Wish for." *Asian Survey*, 48(3): 373–392.

Levitsky, Steven, and Daniel Ziblatt. 2018. *How Democracies Die*. New York: Broadway Books.

Levitsky, Steven and Lucan Way. 2010. *Competitive Authoritarianism: Hybrid Regimes after the Cold War*. Cambridge: Cambridge University Press.

Likhit Dhiravegin. 1988. "Demi-democracy and the Market Economy: The Case of Thailand." *Asian Journal of Social Science*, 16(1): 1–25.

Marinov, N. and H. Goemans. 2014. "Coups and Democracy." *British Journal of Political Science*, 44(4): 799–825.

McCargo, Duncan. 2005. "Network Monarchy and Legitimacy Crises in Thailand." *The Pacific Review*, 18(4): 499–519.

McCargo, Duncan. 2019. "We are grown-up now and can choose for ourselves." *New York Times*. March 29 www.nytimes.com/2019/03/29/opinion/thailand-election-thanathorn-future-forward-youth-vote.html (accessed December 1, 2021).

McCargo, Duncan. 2021. "Network Monarchy as Euphoric Couplet." *Pacific Affairs*, 94(3): 549–565.

McCargo, Duncan and Anyarat Chattharakul. 2020. *Future Forward: The Rise and Fall of a Thai Political Party*. Copenhagen: NIAS Press.

McCargo, Duncan and Ukrist Pathmanand. 2005. *The Thaksinisation of Thailand*. Copenhagen: NIAS Press.

McCoy, Alfred, (ed.). 1993. *An Anarchy of Families: State and Family in the Philippines*. Madison, WI: University of Wisconsin Center for Southeast Asian Studies.

McCoy, Jennifer, Tahmina Rahman, and Murat Somer. 2018. "Polarization and the Global Crisis of Democracy: Common Patterns, Dynamics, and Pernicious Consequences for Democratic Polities." *American Behavioral Scientist*, 62(1): 16–42.

Mérieau, Eugénie. 2016. "Thailand's Deep State, Royal Power and the Constitutional Court (1997–2015)." *Journal of Contemporary Asia*, 46(3): 445–466.

Montesano, Michael, Pavin Chachavalponqpun, and Aekapol Chongvilaivan, (eds.). 2012. *Bangkok, May 2010*: *Perspectives on a Divided Thailand*. Singapore: Institute of Southeast Asian Studies.

Mudde, Cas and Cristóbal Rovira Kaltwasser. 2018. "Studying Populism in Comparative Perspective: Reflections on the Contemporary and Future Research Agenda." *Comparative Political Studies*, 51(13): 1667–1693.

Murashima, Eiji, Nakharin Mektrairat, and Somkiat Wanthana. 1991. *The Making of Modern Thai Political Parties*. Tokyo: IDE.

Nam, Illan and Viengrat Nethipo. 2021. "Building Programmatic Linkages in the Periphery: The Case of the TRT Party in Thailand." *Politics & Society*, 50(3) (September): 1–42.

Naruemon Thabchumpon. 2016. "Contending Political Networks: A Study of the 'Yellow Shirts' and 'Red Shirts' Thailand's Politics." *Southeast Asian Studies*, 5(1): 93–113.

Nattapol Chaiching. 2020. ขุนศึก ศักดินา และพญาอินทรี [Warlord, Royalist, and the Eagle]. Bangkok: Same Sky Book.

Nelson, Michael. 2002. "Thailand's House Elections of 6 January 2001: Thaksin's Landslide Victory and Subsequent Narrow Escape." In *Thailand's New Politics: KPI Yearbook 2001*, edited by Michael Nelson, pp. 283–441. Nonthaburi: King Prajadhipok's Institute.

Nishizaki, Yoshinori. 2011. *Political Authority and Provincial Identity in Thailand: The Making of Banharn-buri*. Ithaca, NY: Cornell University.

Nishizaki, Yoshinori. 2019. "Ironic Political Reforms: Elected Senators, Party-List MPs, and Family Rule in Thailand." *Critical Asian Studies*, 51(2): 210–231.

Noppanan Wannathepsakun. 2006. "Kosang Kanmueang Kanmueang Kosang." [Constructing Politics, Politics of Construction] In *Kan tosu khong thun thai lem 2* [The Struggle of Thai Capital, Vol. 2], edited by Pasuk Phongpaichit, pp. 280–357. Bangkok: Matichon.

Nostitz, Nick. 2009. *Red VS. Yellow*. Bangkok: White Lotus.

Nostitz, Nick. 2014. "The red shirts from anti-coup protestors to social mass movement." In *"Good coup" gone bad: Thailand's political developments since Thaksin's downfall*, edited by Chachavalpongpun Pavin, pp. 170–198. Singapore: Institute of Southeast Asian Studies.

O' Donnell, Guillermo, Philippe Schmitter, and Laurence Whitehead. 1986. *Transitions from Authoritarian Rule: Tentative Conclusions about Uncertain Democracies*. Baltimore, MD: Johns Hopkins University Press.

Ockey, James. 1992. "Business Leaders, Gangsters, and the Middle Class: Societal Groups and Civilian Rule in Thailand," PhD dissertation, Ithaca, NY: Cornell University.

Ockey, James. 1993. "Chaopho: Capital Accumulation and Social Welfare in Thailand." *Crossroads*, 8: 48–77.

Ockey, James. 2000. "The Rise of Local Power in Thailand: Provincial Crime, Elections, and the Bureaucracy." In *Money and Power in Provincial Thailand*, edited by Ruth McVey, pp. 74–96. Singapore: Institute of Southeast Asian Studies.

Pasuk Phongpaichit and Chris Baker. 1995. *Thailand: Economy and Politics*. Kuala Lumpur: Oxford University Press.

Pasuk Phongpaichit and Chris Baker. 2004. *Thaksin: The Business of Politics in Thailand*. Chiang Mai: Silkworm Books.

Pasuk Phongpaichit and Chris Baker. 2005. *A History of Thailand*. Cambridge: Cambridge University Press.

Pasuk Phongpaichit and Chris Baker. 2009. "Thaksin's Populism." In *Populism in Asia*, edited by Kosuke Mizuno and Pasuk Phongpaichit, pp. 66–93. Singapore: NUS Press.

Pasuk Phongpaichit and Chris Baker. 2012. “Thailand in Trouble: Revolt of the Downtrodden or Conflict among Elites?” In *Bangkok, May 2010: Perspectives on a Divided Thailand*, edited by Michael Montesano, Pavin Chachavalponqpun, and Aekapol Chongvilaivan, pp. 214–229. Singapore: Institute of Southeast Asian Studies.

Pasuk Phongpaichit, Sungsidh Piriyarangsan, and Nualnoi Treerat. 1998. *Guns, Girls, Gambling, Ganja: Thailand's Illegal Economy and Public Policy.* Chiang Mai: Silkworm Books.

Pavin Chachavalpongpun, (ed.). 2020. *Coup, King, Crisis: A Critical Interregnum in Thailand.* New Haven, CT: Yale University Council on Southeast Asia Studies.

People's Information Center. 2012. Khwamching phuea khwamyutitham: Het kan lae phonkrathop chak kan salai kan chumnum me sa phruetsa pha 53 [Truth for Justice: the April-May 2010 Crackdown]. Bangkok: PIC.

Pinkaew Laungaramsri. 2016. “Mass Surveillance and the Militarization of Cyberspace in Post-Coup Thailand.” *ASEAS – Austrian Journal of South-East Asian Studies*, 9(2): 195–214.

Porphant Ouyyanont. 2008. “The Crown Property Bureau in Thailand and the Crisis of 1997.” *Journal of Contemporary Asia*, 38(1): 166–189.

Prajak Kongkirati. 2008. “Counter-movements in Democratic Transition: Thai Right-Wing Movements after the 1973 Popular Uprising.” *Asian Review*, 19(1): 101–34.

Prajak Kongkirati. 2012. “Thailand: The Cultural Politics of Student Resistance.” In *Student Activism in Asia: Between Protest and Powerlessness*, edited by Meredith Weiss and Edward Aspinall, pp. 229–258. Minneapolis, MN: University of Minnesota Press.

Prajak, Kongkirati. 2013. “Bosses, Bullets, and Ballots: Electoral Violence and Democracy in Thailand 1975–2011.” PhD dissertation, Australian National University, Canberra.

Prajak, Kongkirati. 2014. “The Rise and Fall of Electoral Violence in Thailand: Changing Rules, Structures and Power Landscapes, 1997–2011.” *Contemporary Southeast Asia*, 36(3): 386–416.

Prajak Kongkirati. 2016a. “Thailand's Political Future Remains Uncertain.” *ISEAS Perspective, 24,* www.iseas.edu.sg/images/pdf/ISEAS_Perspective_2016_42.pdf (accessed October 5, 2021).

Prajak, Kongkirati. 2016b. “Thailand's Failed 2014 Election: The Anti-election Movement, Violence and Democratic Breakdown.” *Journal of Contemporary Asia*, 46(3): 467–485.

Prajak Kongkirati. 2016c. "Evolving Power of Provincial Political Families in Thailand: Dynastic Power, Party machine and Ideological Politics." *South East Asia Research*, 24(3): 386–406.

Prajak Kongkirati. 2018. "Haunted Past, Uncertain Future: The Fragile Transition to Military-Guided Semi-Authoritarianism in Thailand." In *Southeast Asian Affairs*, edited by Malcolm Cook and Daljit Singh, pp. 382–395 . Singapore: ISEAS-Yusof Ishak Institute.

Prajak Kongkirati. 2019a. "Why Thailand's generals fail to co-opt elections." *New Mandala*, January 15, www.newmandala.org/why-thailands-generals-fail-to-co-opt-elections/ (accessed 5 October 2021).

Prajak Kongkirati. 2019b. "Palang Pracharat Party: Can old tricks win in a new political landscape?" *New Mandala*, March 23, www.newmandala.org/palang-pracharat-party-can-old-tricks-win-in-a-new-political-landscape/ (accessed 5 October 2021).

Prajak Kongkirati. 2019c. "Murder and Regress: Violence and Political Change in Thailand." In *After the Coup: The National Council for Peace and Order Era and the Future of Thailand*, edited by Michael Montesano, Terence Chong and Mark Shu Xun Heng, pp. 194–223. Singapore: ISEAS–Yusof Ishak Institute.

Prajak Kongkirati. 2019d. "Overview: Political Earthquakes." *Contemporary Southeast Asia*, 41(2); 163–169.

Prajak Kongkirati. 2019e. "From Illiberal Democracy to Military Authoritarianism: Intra-elite Struggle and Mass-based Conflict in Deeply Polarized Thailand." *The ANNALS of the American Academy of Political and Social Science*, 681(1): 24–40.

Prajak Kongkirati. 2023. "Power without the Polls: Thai-style Authoritarian Fragility amid the Defeat of Military-backed Parties." *Contemporary Southeast Asia*, 45(3): 406–413.

Prajak Kongkirati and Veerayooth Kanchoochat. 2018. "The Prayuth Regime: Embedded Military and Hierarchical Capitalism in Thailand." *TRaNS: Trans - Regional and - National Studies of Southeast Asia*, 6(2): 279–305.

Puangchon Unchanam. 2019. *Royal Capitalism: Wealth, Class, and Monarchy in Thailand*. Madison, WI: The University of Wisconsin Press.

Puangthong Pawakapan. 2021. *Infiltrating Society: The Thai Milita'y's Internal Security Affairs*. Singapore: ISEAS–Yusof Ishak Institute.

Ratcliffe, Rebecca and Navaon Siradapuvadol. 2023. "Thailand's Winning Candidate for PM Blocked From Power," *The Guardian*, July 13, 2023. www.theguardian.com/world/2023/jul/13/winning-thailand-candidate-for-pm-blocked-from-power-pita-limjaroenrat

Reno, William. 1998. *Warlord Politics and African States*. Boulder, CO: Lynner Rienner.

Ricks, Jacob. 2019. "Thailand's 2019 Vote: The General's Election." *Pacific Affairs*, 92(3): 443–457.

Riggs, Fred. 1966. *Thailand: The Modernization of a Bureaucratic Polity.* Honolulu, HI: East- West Center Press.

Roberts, Kenneth. 2006. "Populism, Political Conflict, and Grass-Roots Organization in Latin America." *Comparative Politics*, 36(2): 127–48.

Saowanee Alexander. 2021. "Sticky Rice in the Blood: Isan People's Involvement in Thailand's 2020 Anti-government Protests." *Critical Asian Studies*, 53(2): 219–232.

Schaffar, Wolfram. 2016. "New Social Media and Politics in Thailand: The Emergence of Fascist Vigilante Groups on Facebook." *ASEAS – Austrian Journal of South-East Asian Studies*, 9(2): 215–234.

Schedler, Andreas. 2002 "Elections without Democracy: The Menu of Manipulation." *Journal of Democracy*, 13(2): 36–50.

Selway, Joel and Allen Hicken. 2019. "The Fate of Pheu Thai in the 2019 Elections." *Thai Data Points*, April 11, 2019, www.thaidatapoints.com/post/the-fate-of-pheu-thai-in-the-2019-elections (accessed May 5, 2021).

Siffin, William J. 1966. *Thai Bureaucracy: Institutional Change and Development*. Honolulu, HI: East-West Center Press.

Siripan Nogsuan. 2006. *Thai Political Parties in the Age of Reform*. Bangkok: Institute of Public Policy Studies.

Siripan Nogsuan. 2018. "A Tale of Two Hybrid Regimes: A Study of Cabinets and Parliaments in Indonesia and Thailand." *Japanese Journal of Political Science*, 19(2): 269–292.

Siripan Nogsuan. 2020. "Electoral Integrity and the Repercussions of Institutional Manipulations: The 2019 General Election in Thailand." *Asian Journal of Comparative Politics*, 5(1): 52–68.

Skinner, G. William. 1957. *Chinese Society in Thailand: An Analytical History.* Ithaca, NY: Cornell University Press.

Sombat Chantornvong. 2000. "Local Godfathers in Thai Politics." In *Money and Power in Provincial Thailand*, edited by Ruth McVey, pp. 53–73. Singapore: Institute of Southeast Asian Studies.

Somchai Phatharathananunth. 2008. "The Thai Rak Thai Party and Elections in North-eastern Thailand." *Journal of Contemporary Asia*, 38(1): 106–123.

Somchai Phatharathananunth. 2020. "Dances with Dictators: NGOs and Military Regime in Thailand." In *Coup, King, Crisis: A Critical Interregnum in Thailand*, edited by Pavin Chachavalpongpun, pp. 339–362. New Haven, CT: Yale University Council on Southeast Asia Studies.

Sopranzetti, Claudio. 2012. "Burning Red Desires: Isan Migrants and the Politics of Desire in Contemporary Thailand." *South East Asia Research* 20(3): 361–379.

Sopranzetti, Claudio. 2018. *Owners of the Map: Motorcycle Taxi Drivers, Mobility, and Politics in Bangkok.* Oakland, CA: University of California Press.

Streckfuss, David. 2020. "Lese-majeste within Thailand's Regime of Intimidation." In *Routledge Handbook of Contemporary Thailand*, edited by Pavin Chachavalpongpun, pp. 134–144. New York: Routledge.

Suehiro, Akira. 1989. *Capital Accumulation in Thailand 1855–1985*. Tokyo: Centre for East Asian Cultural Studies.

Supalak Ganjanakhundee. 2022. *A Soldier King: Monarchy and Military in the Thailand of Rama X.* Singapore: ISEAS–Yusof Ishak Institute.

Surachart Bamrungsuk. 2019. "Thaila'd's Zigzag Road to Democracy: Continuity and Change in Military Intervention." In *After the Coup: The National Council for Peace and Order Era and the Future of Thailand*, edited by Michael Montesano, Terence Chong and Mark Shu Xun Heng, pp. 170–193. Singapore: ISEAS–Yusof Ishak Institute.

Thak Chaloemtiarana. 1979. *Thailand: The Politics of Despotic Paternalism.* Bangkok: Social Science Association of Thailand.

Thanee Chaiwat and Pasuk Phongpaichit. 2008. "Rents and Rent-Seeking in the Thaksin Era." In *Thai Capital after the 1997 Crisis*, edited by Pasuk Phongpaichit and Chris Baker, pp. 249–266. Chiang Mai: Silkworm Books.

Thanet Charoenmuang. 2019. "The Red Shirts and their Democratic Struggle in Northern Thailand, April 2010–May 2015." In *After the Coup: The National Council for Peace and Order Era and the Future of Thailand*, edited by Michael Montesano, Terence Chong and Mark Shu Xun Heng, pp. 114–139. Singapore: ISEAS–Yusof Ishak Institute.

Thaweeporn Kummetha. 2013. "Red shirts' mixed thoughts on Pheu Thai and amnesty bill appear at protest." *Prachatai English*, November 10. https://prachataienglish.com/node/3740.

Tita Sanglee. 2022. "Prayut's Popularity Plunges Further, But the Thai Public Can't Name a Better Option," *The Diplomat*, January 5, 2022. https://thediplomat.com/2022/01/prayuts-popularity-plunges-further-but-the-thai-public-cant-name-a-better-option/.

Thompson, Mark. 2019. "Southeast Asia's Troubling Elections: Is there a Silver Lining?" *Journal of Democracy*, 30(4): 149–157.

Thongchai Winichakul. 2008. "Toppling Democracy." *Journal of Contemporary Asia*, 38(1): 11–37.

Thongchai, Winichakul. 2016. *Thailand's Hyper-royalism: Its Past Success and Present Predicament, Trends in Southeast Asia No.7*. Singapore: Institute of Southeast Asian Studies.

Thongchai Winichakul. 2020. *Moments of Silence: The Unforgetting of the October 6, 1976, Massacre in Bangkok*. Honolulu, HI: University of Hawai'i Press.

Ueda, Yoko. 1995. *Local Economy and Entrepreneurship in Thailand: A Case Study of Nakhon Ratchasima*. Kyoto: Kyoto University Press.

Ukrist Pathmanand and Michael Connors. 2019. "Thailand's Public Secret: Military Wealth and the State." *Journal of Contemporary Asia*, 51(2): 278–302.

Ünaldi, Serhat. 2014. "Working Towards the Monarchy and its Discontents: Anti-royal Graffiti in Downtown Bangkok." *Journal of Contemporary Asia*, 44(3): 377–403.

Unger, Danny. 2012. "Flying Blind." In *Bangkok, May 2010: Perspectives on a Divided Thailand*, edited by Michael Montesano, Pavin Chachavalponqpun, and Aekapol Chongvilaivan, pp. 313–322. Singapore: Institute of Southeast Asian Studies.

Veerayooth Kanchoochat. 2016. "Reign-seeking and the Rise of the Unelected in Thailand." *Journal of Contemporary Asia*, 46(3): 486–503.

Viengrat Nethipo. 2008. "Chiang Mai: Family Business, Tourism, and Politics." In *Thai Capital after the 1997 Crisis*, edited by Pasuk Phongpaichit and Chris Baker, pp. 215–234. Chiang Mai: Silkworm Books.

Viengrat Nethipo. 2019. "Thailand's Politics of Decentralization: Reform and Resistance Before and After the May 2014 Coup." In *After the Coup: The National Council for Peace and Order Era and the Future of Thailand*, edited by Michael J Montesano, Terence Chong, and Mark Heng Shu Xun, pp. 224–253. Singapore: ISEAS-Yusof Ishak Institute.

Walker, Andrew. 2012. *Thailand's Political Peasants: Power in the Modern Rural Economy*. Madison, WI: University of Wisconsin Press.

Weinstein, Jeremy. 2006. *Inside Rebellion: The Politics of Insurgent Violence*. Cambridge: Cambridge University Press.

World Bank. 2022. *Thailand Rural Income Diagnostic: Challenges and Opportunities for Rural Farmers*. Bangkok: World Bank.

Yoshifumi, Tamada. 2009. "Democracy and Populism in Thailand." In *Populism in Asia*, edited by Kosuke Mizuno and Pasuk Phongpaichit, pp. 94–111. Singapore: NUS Press.

Cambridge Elements

Politics and Society in Southeast Asia

Edward Aspinall
Australian National University

Edward Aspinall is a professor of politics at the Coral Bell School of Asia-Pacific Affairs, Australian National University. A specialist of Southeast Asia, especially Indonesia, much of his research has focused on democratisation, ethnic politics and civil society in Indonesia and, most recently, clientelism across Southeast Asia.

Meredith L. Weiss
University at Albany, SUNY

Meredith L. Weiss is Professor of Political Science at the University at Albany, SUNY. Her research addresses political mobilization and contention, the politics of identity and development, and electoral politics in Southeast Asia, with particular focus on Malaysia and Singapore.

About the Series

The Elements series Politics and Society in Southeast Asia includes both country-specific and thematic studies on one of the world's most dynamic regions. Each title, written by a leading scholar of that country or theme, combines a succinct, comprehensive, up-to-date overview of debates in the scholarly literature with original analysis and a clear argument.

Cambridge Elements

Politics and Society in Southeast Asia

Elements in the Series

The Politics of Rights and Southeast Asia
Lynette J. Chua

Urban Development in Southeast Asia
Rita Padawangi

Islam and Political Power in Indonesia and Malaysia: The Role of Tarbiyah and Dakwah in the Evolution of Islamism
Joseph Chinyong Liow

Civil Society in Southeast Asia: Power Struggles and Political Regimes
Garry Rodan

The Meaning of Democracy in Southeast Asia: Liberalism, Egalitarianism and Participation
Diego Fossati and Ferran Martinez i Coma

Organized Labor in Southeast Asia
Teri L. Caraway

The Philippines: From 'People Power' to Democratic Backsliding
Mark R. Thompson

Contesting Social Welfare in Southeast Asia
Andrew Rosser and John Murphy

The Politics of Cross-Border Mobility in Southeast Asia
Michele Ford

Myanmar: A Political Lexicon
Nick Cheesman

Courts and Politics in Southeast Asia
Bjoern Dressel

Thailand: Contestation, Polarization, and Democratic Regression
Prajak Kongkirati

A full series listing is available at: www.cambridge.org/ESEA

For EU product safety concerns, contact us at Calle de José Abascal, 56–1°, 28003 Madrid, Spain or eugpsr@cambridge.org.

www.ingramcontent.com/pod-product-compliance
Ingram Content Group UK Ltd.
Pitfield, Milton Keynes, MK11 3LW, UK
UKHW022145080726
473066UK00010B/779

* 9 7 8 1 1 0 8 4 6 5 0 1 4 *